PEER PRESSURE

Campus Life Books

PEER PRESSURE

Making it work for you!

CHRIS LUTES

A DIVISION OF CTi
CampusLife BOOKS / ZondervanPublishingHouse
Grand Rapids, Michigan
A Division of HarperCollinsPublishers

Peer Pressure:
Making it Work for You
Copyright © 1990 by Campus Life Books, a division of CTi
All rights reserved

Published by Zondervan Publishing House
1415 Lake Drive, S.E., Grand Rapids, Michigan 49506

Library of Congress Cataloging-in-Publication Data

Lutes, Chris.
    Peer pressure : making it work for you / Chris Lutes.
      p. cm.
    ISBN 0-310-71111-8
    1. Peer pressure in adolescence—United States. 2. Self-help
techniques. 3. Youth—United States—Religious life. 4. Religious
HQ799.2.P44L87   1990
305.23'5—dc20   90–41281
                                                        CIP

Printed in the United States of America

   91 92 93 94 / CH / 5 4 3 2 1

CONTENTS

INTRODUCTION

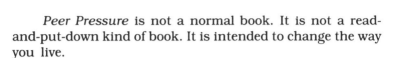

Peer Pressure is not a normal book. It is not a read-and-put-down kind of book. It is intended to change the way you live.

How?

Through keeping a journal. Every so often you will come across a page entitled, *Journal entry.* On it you'll find a few simple questions or instructions. They're meant to make you think, evaluate, even act regarding your world. You can write your responses right in this book, or get a notebook and keep your answers in there. (It's more private, for one thing. And then somebody else can use the book.)

You can read the book without taking the time to do the journal entries. But if you do, you'll miss out. Why? Because negative peer pressure is an active thing. "Hey, do you want to . . . ?" "Hey, why don't you want to come?" If you want to deal with an active pressure, you have to make an active response. That's what this book will help you do.

But you're not going to learn about just negative peer pressure. You are going to discover *positive* peer pressure. That's right, peer pressure can be positive. You can use peer pressure to do good things for yourself, for your friends, and for your peers. Start reading to discover how.

Fitting In

Where Do I Fit In?

LONGING TO BELONG

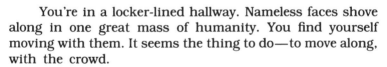

Peer pressure starts with a deep, fundamental human longing—the longing to belong. Everybody wants to be accepted, to fit in. That longing leads to peer groups, which lead (inevitably) to peer pressure.

You're in a locker-lined hallway. Nameless faces shove along in one great mass of humanity. You find yourself moving with them. It seems the thing to do—to move along, with the crowd.

Safe.

You find that it's comfortable being caught up in the stream, in the rush and rumbling of others—but eventually you tire of moving with the crowd. So homogeneous. So monotonous.

So boring.

You exit, meandering down another hallway. You seek a few people who are like you. But who are you? You don't know. You're beginning to feel alone. You need someone. You need to belong.

You need to fit in.

Suddenly one person, and then another, appear. Some have hair clipped to the scalp. Others have long hair that is

PEER PRESSURE

moussed into green, blue, and orange spikes. Some carry tons of books and notebooks proudly tucked under their arms. There are strong, muscular types. Attractive, bouncy cheerleader types.

Types.

They begin to pair up, kind attracting kind, attaching themselves to each other like Velcro strips on shoes. First a pair here. Then three, four there. Grouping up. Suddenly a group of letter-jacket types moves along with a purpose: attracting the bouncy cheerleader types. Then some wild-looking characters all dressed in clothes that look like rock 'n' roll advertisements saunter down their own path, turning into a room marked "Burnouts." A band of cheerleaders somersaults down the hall, shaking pom-poms and showing toothy smiles. They skip into a room labeled "Rah-rahs." The letter jackets follow. With a purpose.

On it goes.

Suddenly there's you. Where do you fit in? In your own group. There they are, over there. Ah, security. Finally. A round peg fitting snugly in that perfectly circular slot. But do you really fit?

Or are you like Trey?

Tonight my football team, the Lytle Pirates, won the district championship. Since this is my senior year, nothing could be more exciting to me. I can just feel the electricity in the air.

Right now the whole team is out having a good time— gettin' rowdy. As a member of the Lytle Pirates, I should be out with them, having the time of my life. But I'm not. Earlier this evening I looked down at the cast on my broken foot and thought, You know, since I haven't been able to play for the last five games, I've been more or less ostracized by the rest of the team.

I noticed it even at the pep rally this afternoon. The band started playing the school song, signaling all the seniors out onto the gym floor. Of course, I went out with the rest. The football players were on one side hugging each other and singing—forming their own private huddle. The cheerleaders were grabbing the better players. I was sort of left out. I felt embarrassed being in front of three hundred students with my senior class, and standing behind the huddle.

So I edged up close to my football friends and tried to bring up an old private joke. They laughed for a second and then got back to their private huddle. Suddenly I began to see what it feels like not to be a part of the most popular group in school.

These are supposed to be my friends. They are the school's in-crowd. I have struggled through football just to be a part of this group. Now I am punted out. Why? Just because I hurt my leg?

Trey had worked hard to get into the fast lane of the team. He practiced. He sweated. He "clean and jerked" tons of weights. For what? To belong. To be in the most popular group. In the in-crowd. But now he was out. Dumped.

Popularity. Groups. In-crowds. One day at the top, the next day back wandering the halls, wondering what happened. Is belonging—fitting in—worth the hassle?

NEW KID IN TOWN

You're a freshman. Or you've switched schools. You're sitting at home, in your room, staring at your poster of U2. *What if the kids at this school don't like U2?* you think to yourself. *What if the kids at this new school don't like me?* Your anxieties keep you awake. Through the Late Show; through the Late, Late Show; through Morning Exercises with Francis Fitness. You wonder, over and over: *Will I fit in anywhere?*

So did Mike.

The summer before I started high school I had a lot of fears about making friends. And that's why I got involved with Ed's group.

Ed, who lives down the street, was my first "real" high-school friend. At that time he was going to be a junior and I, the soon-to-be freshman, looked up to him. I was willing to do just about anything to be a part of Ed's group. So that summer Ed gave me an education about his definition of fun times—and an education about his understanding of friendship.

Ed's idea of a good time with friends was sitting around smoking marijuana. I remember the first night I got stoned. About two houses down from where I live there's a ditch between two houses. Ed and I went back there and he showed me a bong filled with Sprite. We lit up.

That was just the beginning. As the summer went on I was stoned more than I was together. We smoked up every day. When school started in the fall, we kept right on smoking. We were wasted most of the time, so a lot of the things I did during that time are pretty fuzzy.

One thing I do remember was stealing. We'd go into grocery stores and drugstores and take junk food and cigarettes. Again, this was Ed's idea of a good time. I was never sure about doing this, but I couldn't refuse. I wanted to fit in with my group of friends.

Mike got caught stealing. He had a couple of cigarette cartons stuck down his pant leg. He was humiliated. All because he wanted to please Ed and his cronies. He'd wasted a summer being wasted. All because he needed that special friendship, that special peer group.

What about Ed? Well, when Mike got caught with the goods, Ed got caught with nothing. Not one smoke. Sure, he pushed Mike into ripping off grocery stores. But when push came to risk—Ed left the hard part to Mike. Some friend. Some peer. Is this what friendship is all about?

DUMPED

You've spent so much time with your best friend, she's like a sister. But unlike a sister, you two agree on everything: hairstyle, clothing style, music style. You can't think of anybody better, anybody closer. You'd do anything for her.

Deena had a friend like that.

A few months back, I piled into a friend's '76 Caddie along with my best friend, Barb, and four other girls. We were headed for the big annual rodeo held at the San Antonio Convention Center. This rodeo is a major, all-day event—with carnival rides and the works.

So there we were on the way to one of the biggest events of the year—and I sensed this bad feeling in the air. It was as though my friends were saying, "Deena, you're not really one of us." I must explain that the feeling didn't just begin in the car. A couple of weeks earlier I had overheard the other girls talking about going to the rodeo, and, almost as a passing thought, Barb said to me, "Oh, do you want to go?" Barb hadn't even planned on inviting me in the first place. My best friend!

We had been drifting apart for quite awhile. I guess it had a lot to do with our lifestyles. Barb and many of our other friends like to party—to drink and stuff like that. But partying makes me uncomfortable. I was raised in a pretty moral home and my grandfather is a minister. As a Christian, I just felt certain things were wrong, but my friends didn't see it that way. We'd had some fairly heated discussions about our differences, so I think they'd been starting to nudge me to the outer edge of their circle. But I didn't realize how much they, and Barb, had wanted me out—until the rodeo.

When we finally got to the Rodeo Center, Barb dashed

off to go on some rides with three of the other girls. This left me and another girl pretty much by ourselves.

I like this other girl, but what bothered me was that Barb had just taken off without me—not seeming to care what I wanted to do. Sure I was jealous: Here were some

YES, MOM, THE STRIPE.... NO WAIT... WHY CAN'T SHE MAKE UP HER MIND?

other people grabbing my best friend's attention. But mostly I was hurt. Even with our differences, I'd thought we were too close to split up.

The fickle freestyle of friendship. Deena on the outs. Somebody else on the ins. Why? In Deena's case, she had different morals than Barb and the rest. So it was "So long, Deena." Isn't there room for friends to be different, and still be friends?

MAKING THE GRADE

Dreams. You have dreams of belonging—to that special group. You know it's a good group, one of the best. Your parents even say so. Your friends admire anybody who's in it. It takes a lot of work to get in and stay in. You gotta keep those grades up. You gotta make special meetings and practices. All to get in. All to stay in.

Shannon "got in"—sort of.

I'm a sophomore flag twirler for the MacArthur High School Brahma Bulls. When I joined the team I was really excited.

To explain, let me tell a little about the team and their outfits. Each girl carries a six-foot pole with a white-striped blue banner attached to it. On the end of the triangular-shaped banner is a long silver strip of cloth—which really whips around when you make quick movements. Each twirler wears white boots, royal blue culottes, and a blue-striped white blouse with puffy sleeves. The uniform also has a large satin bow tie. Topping it all off is a white cowboy hat with one side tacked up and a long plume in the band.

It's all very colorful and neat—especially when the flag team is synchronized with the marching band. As a matter of fact, both the band and the flag team won first place last year in state competition.

Added to all of these attractions was the fact that some of my friends from church were twirlers. One of the girls from my youth group was even the colonel—the highest-ranking person on the team. This girl kept telling me how much fun twirling was. It didn't take a lot to convince me. I could hardly think of anything more exciting than being a part of this elite group. The following spring I went out for tryouts and made it.

Then my troubles began. There were thirty-eight of us on the team, but only thirty-two could perform on the football field. The rest served as alternates (a nice term for being stuck on the bench). I was an alternate.

The first couple of games, I wasn't too upset about not performing. But as the season went on, and I didn't get to march, I became more and more discouraged. I even cried during morning practices.

Sure, I wore the uniform, but I still didn't really belong.

Dreams. Nightmares. Are they one and the same when it comes to fitting in? All that hard work to get on the honor roll, to make the varsity squad, to be a cheerleader, to be a debate team captain—to be a part of a special peer group. Is it worth it?

Popularity vs. coldness. Couple that conflict with the need to fit in, and you feel like you'll do anything to belong. But let one thing go wrong—break one foot—and out you go.

However, there is a flip side to this long-playing record called peer pressure. It's a good side. It's where peer pressure becomes a force for good.

Remember Trey? Before he got pushed to the outer edges of the football players—before he broke his foot—he spent a day with David.

There was this one day when I worked with David out in the hay field. I was into the football in-crowd. David wasn't. He never had been.

David's a nerd. Well, that's what the in-crowd calls him and others like him. David won't party, a prerequisite for "in" status. And he sticks pretty close to his religion. We would call him names like "Billy Graham" or "Oral Roberts."

But that day, as the perspiration dripped off my chin in a steady stream, I looked at David up there on the hay wagon and I realized I admired him for his guts. He didn't seem to have any desire to be part of the in-crowd. He was his own man. Now, I claimed to be a Christian myself. But I didn't have David's guts. He refused to drink; I didn't. I couldn't even say no to football—a sport I had never really enjoyed in the first place.

After that day with David, my parents caught me drunk. Things got real tough for a while. After things calmed down at home, I had a chance to do a lot of thinking. My time with David helped stimulate that thinking. It wasn't anything he had said that really changed things. It was just his style. He lived out what he felt was right—inside.

I started saying to myself, "Why should I be pushed around by what others think? Maybe I should try to get involved with other Christians like David."

Right now I'm leaning closer and closer toward the lifestyle a guy's supposed to have as a Christian. I don't want to drink anymore. It's really starting to get to the point where I don't care what the in-crowd is going to say, what the football players think. Even though those guys think nonplayers and straight people are nerds, who's to say the football players and party people aren't the real nerds?

I'm just thankful for guys like David. He helped get me thinking right. Just knowing he can stand up for what *he believes has given me the courage to do the same. People like him help set the pace for people like me.*

David. By simply being a good example, he became a positive influence. Bad peer pressure from the team is countered by good peer pressure from a guy like David. It happened with Trey.

It's not just the exceptional guys, the Davids, who can use positive peer pressure. An entire group can do positive things. They can help; they can make things better for everyone. Take Shannon for instance. A group of her friends on the flag team turned out to be true friends. They didn't reject her; they put their hands on her shoulders and encouraged her along. She stuck it out because a group of friends cared.

Good peer pressure.

Good group peer pressure.

Consider Mike and Deena. Both found another group of friends—and another group of friends found them. These friends, Christian friends, cared about them for who they were as people. Not for their status, their coolness, or their popularity—but for themselves.

Says Mike: "My friends now are real friends, not like Ed. When I need them, they're there. And when they need me, I'm around. It's a two-way kind of friendship."

You are moving down the long hallway. You are Trey. Pushed. Pulled. Jerked around. No, you are David. Or you're one person in Shannon's, Mike's, or Deena's new group of friends. You don't care about what's in, what's cool, what's popular. You do care about people—about individuals. You care about their problems. Even about their obsession with status.

So you let them know you care. No matter what kind of gym shoes they're wearing, whether or not their jackets bear letters. You care about them. As people. As friends.

That's what this book is all about: peer pressure. Yes, it can be bad (we'll talk more about that later), but it can be good, too. It can be a force to build friendships. It can be a force you and your group can use.

JOURNAL entry☑

Write your own definitions!

- **Peer Pressure is** _____

  _____

  _____

- **Friendship is** _____

  _____

  _____

- What's the difference between peer pressure and friendship?

  _____

  _____

Today's Date: _____

Name that group!

Label a circle for every "group" you know. Then inside the circle write the names of your friends and acquaintances who belong to each group. (Yes, some can belong to more than one.)

I've included some samples to get you started . . .

Today's Date: _____

The Social Habit

Michael Hovart with Patrick Shea

THE PRESSURE'S ON

Giving in to group pressure . . . it's like discovering your skin's been dyed hot pink at the beach. You're just out there basking in the good times, soaking up those old rays of friendship, and before you know it—*zap!*—things are out of hand.

Michael was one of those zapped people. His desire to belong, his need to be in that one special group, led to his "social habit."

There was one group in school I always wanted to join. I figured if I could just be friends with those guys, everything would be great. So I started drinking because that's what they did—and I developed what I call my "social habit." That is, I made drinking a habit because I knew it would keep my friends around.

During the summer between my junior and senior

years in high school, I moved away from home and into an apartment. I had no one to answer to and I could do whatever I wanted. So my place became the logical choice for parties. Things were shaping up for a great year. Yet, somehow, I wasn't feeling all that great. I had gained what I thought I wanted socially, but I didn't feel right about having it.

It was as if my apartment and my drinking were buying me what I wanted: acceptance. But I felt uneasy about getting friends that way. I wanted people to accept me as I was, not because I happened to have a convenient place for parties. I wondered if I should quit drinking, especially since it made me real uncomfortable at times. But if I gave it up I would have to gamble my friendships, and I didn't want to risk that.

These mixed feelings pushed to the surface at the first football game of the season. My friends had been notified to meet at my place about 6:30 P.M. They came, along with some other friends, with the beer and wine they had been drinking. Forty of us squeezed into my small apartment and continued drinking until about 7:15 when we left for the game, rowdy and drunk.

On the way to the opposing team's school we stopped at Beverage King and bought some more beer, this time in quart bottles. By the time the game started at 8:00, I had downed a few quarts and was feeling bloated. I was also having difficulty focusing. Things were hazy, out of proportion.

I stood in the stands on the visitor side and squinted so I could see across the field. The home-team stands blurred into a panel of color, but there was a commotion, too. A few intoxicated troublemakers from our school had walked through the only entrance and promptly picked a fight with some guys from our opponents' school. Before long, the fight erupted into a brawl with dozens of students going after those few who had started the whole thing. I

PEER PRESSURE

Although he tried to look cool, it was obvious to the others that Larry had never smoked a sneaker before.

suddenly felt very conspicuous, standing on the visitor side, drunk and dizzy.

The whole opposite side of the field was beginning to look like one massive human wall. About two hundred people were blocking the only exit, and they were angry. Smaller fights were breaking out all around. Someone said the guys who started it all had hopped the back fence.

I stood there watching all this, and in my alcohol-muddled brain, I was just sure I'd be the next guy to get messed up. I felt too queasy to be heroic; I had that hopeless feeling you get when you are sure something is totally out of your control and all you can do is wait to see what will develop. Whether it made sense or not, I kept thinking I would not be so helpless if it weren't for my friends and the beer I had been guzzling earlier that evening.

I got through it okay. But late that night, when I was

alone in my apartment, I started thinking through the whole scene at the football game. It hit me just how wrong and pointless drinking seemed. I began to think that breaking the habit might be worth the effort.

Still, I was concerned about not losing face with my friends, so I manufactured a convenient excuse to use when someone offered me a beer, and I found the willpower to say no. "Well, I'm going out for wrestling" (which I was), "and I'm not supposed to drink" (which I wasn't). But of course, there was a whole lot more to it than that.

Then came the Toga Party, a modern replay of the Roman "orgies." My friend Steve's parents were out of town, so we put together one incredible bash. We printed invitations, charged a few bucks for admission, and required everyone to wear a toga to get in. There was a huge decorated cake and fifteen cases of beer. It was the major status event of the year: If you were invited to Steve's Toga Party, you were in.

But at the party that night I just walked around watching my sheet-clad friends getting more and more drunk. Suddenly I realized that it isn't any fun being the nondrinker at a party where everyone else is boozing it up. *In fact,* I concluded, *if you aren't getting drunk yourself, there is nothing more annoying than someone who is drunk.* That was a new concept to me.

I watched, a casual observer, as my friends got smashed out of their minds. It was a ridiculous, almost eerie sensation. I left early that evening, realizing I had just attended the biggest party of my senior year and I hadn't even had a good time. I was an outsider—a mere spectator.

That same feeling was confirmed a couple of weeks later at a friend's house. It was just a small party, a casual get-together. But I had that same spectator sensation. I was in the crowd, yet isolated; people were all around, yet I was alone.

As I stood there with my hands empty, I felt conspicu-

PEER PRESSURE

ous and awkward. I wanted to do something with my hands, so I grabbed a beer. But I had lost my taste for alcohol over the past few weeks, so I drank only about half of it. I stayed for a little while—alone, quiet—then I left. The half-empty can sat untouched in the beverage holder on the side panel of my car for weeks before I finally dumped it out.

I began to realize that I actually felt uncomfortable with the group that I had done so much to join. I started avoiding the parties and got more honest about my reasons for not drinking. I had become a Christian when I was quite young, but my compromising—my social habit of drinking and partying—had pretty much pushed God aside.

I knew that drinking was not the true conflict; it was merely a surface battle. My hassle with alcohol was an echo of another deeper struggle: the need to be accepted by others. But that habit had become a wedge that drove me and God apart. It was when I was willing to walk back through the crowd, even if it meant being isolated and alone, that I found there are some things more important than "acceptance" by the in-crowd.

Just the Little Things

GROUP PRESSURE

It doesn't always come from the major stuff, as in Michael's big booze-party scene. It invades the small, day-to-day activities of school life—even of the most "moral," model Christians. So it was with Scott and Linda. They were the kind of kids a mother would be proud of. Neither one had problems with sex, booze, or drugs. They both knew how to say no to "those things." But they both had trouble standing up and saying no to the "little stuff." The stuff that hurt others.

Scott: "Jim was the perfect object for a little fun."

It started out as a harmless prank. Jim was, simply put, the classic example of a gullible nerd, the perfect object for a little fun. He desperately wanted to be considered "one of us," and was naive enough to do almost anything we suggested.

I'm not sure whose idea it was to bring the eggs, but we were all pretty sure that Jim would not disappoint us. If we told him it was macho to down a dozen raw eggs, he'd do it.

I sat near the end of the cafeteria table amid the

lunchtime commotion as Howard cracked the eggs into an empty jar. He pulled out a spoon with a flourish and whipped the eggs, into a thick, yellow, paint-like liquid. Jim looked on with anticipation, almost eagerness, sure that this simple rite would make him one of us.

The jar was passed, almost ceremoniously, to Jim, who pushed his thick glasses back up his sloping nose. As he wrapped his fingers around the jar, we began cheering him on. There was a moment's hesitation as Jim squinted first at the murky mixture and then at us.

"Can I add some juice? It'd help the taste."

"Uh, sure, Jim," Howard assured him. "Whatever you want."

That was all the encouragement Jim needed. Having added a splash of juice to the concoction, he raised the jar to his lips, threw his head back and guzzled it down, turning greener by the gulp. This done, Jim slipped the empty jar onto the table, collapsed into a chair, then began vomiting up the whole ghastly brew.

As Jim was ushered to the nurse's office, our good humor turned sour. A few minutes later, when the assistant principal entered the cafeteria and stepped up to our table, we grew silent. All he said was, "Put yourself in Jim's shoes and ask yourself how you'd be feeling right now." For me, that was all that needed to be said.

I would think again before I allowed myself to just sit and watch while my friends hurt somebody else. It would be hard going against the crowd, but I decided then and there not to let something like this happen again.

Linda: "I felt uneasy about cheating on Kurz's assignment."

Mr. Kurz was still droning on about the weekend assignment when the bell called a halt to another grueling calculus class. I quickly jotted down his unrealistic expectations on a scrap of notebook paper, slammed my calc book shut, and leaped out of my chair. Friday, finally—and I had plans. I filed Kurz's assignment into the great recess of my mind called "I'll Get It Done Somehow . . . Later."

When I stepped through the crowd and out into the sunlight, my friend Julie walked up and remarked, "Don't worry about this one, Linda. We'll get together Sunday night after youth group and breeze through these ten problems. I'd never figure them out on my own, would you? Who does Kurz think we are, a bunch of geniuses?"

I smiled in agreement but said nothing. I knew Julie had heard Kurz's final instructions as well as I had: "This assignment is to be done on your own. No group projects, please."

I felt a bit uneasy, but I dismissed it with the thought, *Oh, well, I'll cross that bridge when I come to it.*

The bridge came quickly.

As usual, the weekend blurred by in a frenzy of upbeat activity. Then, as Sunday evening rolled around, my mind snapped to attention. The calculus dilemma: Kurz's Curse.

I pulled out my calc text and fumbled with my notebook. Question number one. I bogged down more quickly than I had expected. Time was running out. Within twenty minutes I had to leave for evening church. Afterward, I would have only three hours to complete the assignment.

Then the phone rang. "We're meeting at Karen's house after youth group to do the assignment." It was Julie. "You'll be there, won't you?"

I had hoped Julie would have forgotten so I'd be forced to do the assignment on my own. It would have made the ethical decision easier.

"What about Kurz's instructions to work alone?" I awkwardly remarked, hoping to draw at least some reluctant agreement.

"Come on, Linda, we'll never figure those problems out on our own! We're just gonna pool our resources as people . . . not really cheat in the true sense."

PEER PRESSURE

"Yeah, well . . . uh, I'll probably be there," I replied, postponing the inevitable.

As I hung up, my palms were soaked with sweat. *What am I going to do? What if I don't go?* My stomach tightened.

As I grew more nervous, I berated myself for making such an issue out of nothing. I thought of more involved moral questions and felt foolish for jeopardizing my friendships over something so insignificant. Was there any point in rocking the boat? I made up my mind to go along with the group. Yet I wondered why I didn't feel more at ease, why my stomach still ached, why my palms were still moist.

"Let's get going," Julie called out after youth group that evening. "We've got ten whoppers to crank out for Kurz and I want to be sure they are done, and done right."

I wondered if Julie saw any of the inconsistency in her approach to this assignment. I wondered if anyone else even recognized the predicament I felt. Cheating *is* cheating.

"Some of you can ride with me and the rest can ride with Linda," Julie announced as if she were supervising a work crew. "Is that okay, Linda?" The question sounded like an afterthought.

The moment of truth had come.

"I . . . I think I'm just gonna go home and finish up the assignment. I got started this afternoon and don't have much left." I blurted it out, stretching the truth to the limit.

The silence was thick and heavy as my friends must have been tracing the ethical debate through their own consciences.

"Yeah, well, fine, Linda. Go ahead, Miss Math Wizard. We didn't realize you were so fond of calculus. Are you and Kurz on a first-name basis yet?"

Julie always spoke for the crowd, but I knew the entire group resented my action. I could feel my friends' rejection as unmistakably as if it were something I could pick up and handle.

JOURNAL
entry

A Leader

. . . is someone who motivates a group of people to act in a certain way. He or she may "motivate" others to go to the same school activity, to wear the same kind of shoes, or to laugh at a certain person.

- *In your group* . . . who is a leader?

  1. _____

  2. _____

- *In your group* . . . who is a follower?

  1. _____

  2. _____

- *In your group* . . . what do the "leaders" get the "followers" to do?

  _____

  _____

  _____

Today's Date: _____

PEER PRESSURE

JOURNAL entry

Write a letter

. . . to your "group." If you could say anything to the group of kids you hang out with—if you could influence them in some way for the good—what would you say?

Dear

How to Say No (Nicely)

Verne Becker

FOLLOWING A DIFFERENT DRUMMER

Even the best peer group will sometimes lead in the wrong direction. There's only one appropriate response: say no. But it makes quite a difference *how* you say no.

Can you say no without feeling like a jerk, and without putting down your friends? Here are a few suggestions:

1. *Decide ahead of time what you will and won't do.* If you're headed for a party and you suspect people will be drinking there, settle on an answer *before* you walk in the door and someone shoves a beer into your hand. Or if your friends are going to group up on an assignment that's supposed to be done solo, decide what you are going to say *before* your friends pass out textbooks and pencils. With this advanced planning you won't be caught off guard. You'll also gain a sense of confidence and control over your choices.

2. *Be friendly yet firm.* You'll find that people respect someone who can be an individual without being a snob. Your friendliness and confidence may convince other less-confident bystanders to say no as well.

3. *Be honest.* Something's awry when you have to lie in

PEER PRESSURE

order to avoid doing something you don't think is right. Simply state the truth and leave it at that. If you're sick and tired of your group of friends putting down the class nerd, let them know it. If you don't like beer, say so. If you *do* like it, say, "Looks good, but I think I'll have a Coke instead." If you feel uncomfortable going to an R-rated movie, say so.

4. *Speak for others when they won't speak for themselves.* As we have seen, we can—and should—use peer pressure for good. If your friend is ready to drive drunk, you should do everything you can to get him or her out from behind the wheel. Along with refusing to ride with this person, you should do your best to keep your friend from harming others—including himself or herself. Of if your group is constantly putting someone down, you shouldn't just stand aside and let it happen. Let your displeasure be known—tactfully yet firmly.

One way to deal with this is to suggest an alternative. Push for a different movie, ask for a Coke instead of a beer, initiate a "cram session" the day before the test for anyone who wants to come, subtly move the conversation away from gossip by asking a question about something else. Remember, others may feel the same way you do and may simply need someone to speak up.

5. *Speak for yourself.* There is an exception to almost every rule, including the one above. What if you have tried to get your group to do what is right, but there is no positive response? Do you keep nagging or hassling? No. In the end, you're not responsible for everyone else's actions—only your own. If the others won't respond after you've made your opinion known, don't just shrug your shoulders and keep carrying on. Refuse to be involved in something you believe is wrong.

6. *Affirm the person; reject the action.* If you're getting pressure from friends, assure them that you want to be with them but not when they're doing what you feel is wrong. Separate the activity from the person.

7. *Appeal to laws and rules.* If someone asks you to break the law or to break the stated rules of your school, home, or job, don't feel guilty about saying no. Simply say that you'd rather stick by the rules.

8. *Appeal to possible consequences.* "My parents would kill me if they ever found out I went there!" "I'd rather not risk getting suspended for cheating." "No thanks, I'm driving tonight and don't want to take any chances."

9. *Accept the possibility of rejection.* Even if you decline graciously and don't condemn your friends, someone may feel resentful and snub you. This may hurt, but if you endure the pain and seek out friends who are more accepting, you'll be better off in the long run.

Friendship

What Color Is a Friend?

Paul Harris

ARE YOU INTO COLOR-GROUPING?

So far, the "social habits"—the group pressures we give in to—have been on the personal side: party hassles, putting down the class nerd, cheating. Now we present a story involving a social habit that has infected our entire society, and many other societies as well: racial prejudice. Whether we're black, white, brown, or yellow, color-grouping affects us all.

Maybe your school is all black or all white, so color doesn't seem to be an issue. Still, when was the last time you heard somebody in your school tell an ethnic (Polish, for example) joke? Admit it: There is a problem.

Sometimes I wonder whether black people and white people will ever get along. At my school they don't. Technically we're integrated, but actually black kids hang out with black kids, and white kids hang out with white kids; and everybody is scared.

I guess it all goes back to the civil rights movement. In

the fifties, the people in my town, Birmingham, Alabama, turned dogs and fire hoses on black demonstrators. I don't remember it, of course, but my parents do. And the distrust from that time has been passed down to us kids.

Last fall I started going to my school's Campus Life club. I didn't know much about it, but I was willing to give it a try. I had a good time, so I went back. I kept returning, even though I was the only black kid there.

The club was something any kid, white or black, would enjoy. It's just that, in our school, whites go to some things and blacks attend others. There's not much mixing because when there is, friction usually results. So each club or activity tends to get labeled white or black. Campus Life got labeled white.

That didn't matter too much to me. We're just human beings. My little brother plays with white kids down the street. He doesn't know that they're supposed to be different. Like him, I wasn't going to stop hanging around a fun and very friendly group just because of skin color.

Besides, kids at Campus Life were talking about Christianity in a way I could understand. I began to realize that I could be a Christian and still have a really good time in life. Up to that time my idea of a good time had been mostly going out and stealing, cussing, and fighting—but I'd gotten tired of that. I'd been fighting for a long time and never got anything out of it but bruises and black eyes. What was the point?

I found out that the white kids who went to Campus Life were just normal people, maybe nicer than normal people. I liked them, and it didn't matter what color they were.

My older brother, whom I've always admired, finally told me I should quit. He told me that Campus Life was turning me into a white boy. I asked him, "Are you prejudiced?" He said, "No, man, I just don't want you to go over with all those honkies."

Then my black friends started in on me. They'd push me around and call me names like "Oreo"—you know, black on the outside, but white on the inside. It didn't happen just once or twice—it happened all the time. All the old friends I'd hung around with were suddenly treating me like a traitor.

The threats didn't scare me; I'd just laugh. I knew I could handle those guys if I had to. They weren't any braver or tougher than I was. Nobody could push me around. But I didn't want to lose every friend I had, to end up an outcast just because I insisted on joining some club. Eventually all of this made me think about quitting Campus Life.

A couple of things stopped me. First, the more I learned about Jesus, the better I liked him and the life he offered. Campus Life was helping me understand what Christianity meant. Therefore, Campus Life was important to me.

Second, I began to figure, "If my friends drop me because I go to a meeting they don't like, then they really aren't very good friends. A friend is supposed to accept you the way you are."

Louis, a guy I'd met at Campus Life, was becoming what I'd call a true friend. He accepted me for what I was. Louis was short and muscular—built like a fireplug. One day we were in the gym playing slaphand, a game where you stand an arm's length apart and try to knock each other off balance just by hitting hands. Suddenly there were six black guys beside us. One of them began to hassle Louis, pushing him, wanting to fight. Louis just said he didn't want to fight. But the guy was getting mean. He pulled out a knife and pushed it toward Louis. "I'm going to cut you," he said. Still Louis wouldn't fight.

One of the other guys tried to hand another knife to Louis. "Fight with mine," he said. But Louis wouldn't take it. The first guy looked like he really would try to cut him.

I kept saying, "Put the knife down. There isn't anything to fight over." But he wouldn't listen. So I grabbed his

PEER PRESSURE

STRAIGHT A's, RICO? WE GREASERS HAVE STANDARDS!

arm, seized the knife, and threw it across the gym floor. He held on to me and we tussled and pushed at each other. Finally we broke off. "It's not worth it," I told him. After some threats to both Louis and me, he and the rest of the guys left.

Louis was full of thanks. He'd been scared. I said, "That's okay. You're my friend. I don't stand by and watch when my friends are getting hassled." Then I realized that I had made my choice. I doubt that any time before I would have sided with a white guy against some black guys, no matter who was right. But Louis was a real friend, and real friendship counted more than race.

I got hassled a lot after that—guys wanted to fight me. They'd test me by asking me to go out and do something—smoke some dope, steal some stuff—and when I wouldn't they'd want to know why. "I just don't do that anymore" didn't satisfy them. I lost almost every friend I had. That really hurt, and there were times when I got terribly down.

But gradually the tide turned. My "friends" stopped hassling me, and by the end of the year they saw how I was hanging in there and they began to respect me. Over the summer I went to a Campus Life conference and met some black guys from other cities. We talked about my situation, and I began to see that things could change. I'm hoping pretty soon some of my black friends will begin to come to Campus Life.

In the meantime, I intend to keep on having a good time growing as a Christian. It hasn't been easy. There were some low, lonely times. I suppose anytime you do something really different, really important, you're going to have to go against the stream. That isn't fun, but nobody ever promised it would be. Besides, what kind of life would you have if you only did what everybody else does?

Gangs

Gregg Lewis

GANGS AND PEER PRESSURE

If you live in the suburbs or on R. R. #2, you may be wondering, "What's a story on gangs got to do with the peer pressure I'm experiencing?" While it's true that gang graffiti doesn't get scrawled on most school hallways, there are some interesting—and frightening—similarities between "normal" peer pressure and the pressure gang members put on each other.

As you read the following interview with six Chicago gang members, compare gang pressure with the pressure you experience daily in your own school and community.

Gregg: **How did you get started in gangs?**

Milton: I've been a Puerto Rican Stone since I was eleven. I got started because my older brother was a Stone.

Joey: I got in with gangs when I was nine. The older guys paid me to steal and deliver things for them. It seemed like a great life. I was having fun and making money, too. I worked for a lot of different gangs until one of them thought I was a traitor and beat me up. That's when I joined my neighborhood gang, the Insane Dragons.

James: I joined the Vice Lord peewee organization

when I was ten because my older brothers were all Vice Lords and I needed protection from other gangs who were after my family.

John Patrick: There wasn't any gang in my hood [neighborhood] until I was fourteen. That's when the Latin Kings came in and impressed me with their wine, dine, dance, and song. I saw guys having fun, getting high, making it with girls; I wanted what they had.

David: I've been hassled by gang members all my life. I even transferred from one high school to another to get away from some Simon City Royals who wanted to beat me up. I just wanted to get an education and stay out of trouble; in fact, I had a straight-A average until last year when a bunch of Latin Eagles jumped me because they thought I belonged to the Kings. After that I joined the P. R. Stones for protection and revenge.

Luis: I've always lived right in the middle of the Stones' hood, but I didn't take part in the gang until a year or so ago. I was walking down the third floor hallway of my high school when three Latin Eagles took three shots at me. Ever since that day I've dedicated myself to being a Latin-Eagle killer.

Something very similar happened to a friend of mine named Richard. He was a straight-A student, the starring running back on the varsity football team as a freshman, a track star, and a guy who always minded his own business. But because his four brothers had been Stones, the Eagles hassled him. One day they saw his arms crossed the wrong way, showing the sign of a certain gang, and they threatened to shoot him. He decided to fight back and join a gang; now he's in jail charged with murder.

Gregg: **Why is gang life appealing?**

Joey: Some of the appeal is just fun and excitement. You can get high, make some money.

Milton: The Stones are a family. Besides gang-banging [fighting] with enemy gangs, we love each other. And with a gang on almost every corner, you've got to belong to something. If you walk down the street to Burger King and someone represents to you—shows their gang hand-sign— and you don't respond, they may move on you.

James: I think most people join for protection. Your friends will protect you and your family.

John Patrick: I think when a kid is thirteen or fourteen he needs something to fall back on. He needs to feel good about himself. When he goes with his neighborhood gang to meet with allies from other neighborhoods and sees how many "friends" he has, he thinks, *Wow, we're big and we're bad.*

With all the money and the partying it looks like the open door to a fantasy world. But it often leads to disaster. At this point I have to say that the things gangs stand for are stupid.

Gregg: How have your attitudes toward gangs changed over the years?

David: I didn't see much use for gangs and never wanted to be in one when I was growing up. It wasn't until I needed protection that I began to see all that a gang can mean and do for you.

John Patrick: Going to jail really turned my thinking around. That and spending some time with a cousin who's shown me there's a better way to make it in life than gangs. And I got tired of seeing my mother cry whenever I was locked up.

I can't see anything good about gangs anymore. I used to keep an arsenal of guns under my mattress and I used them on anyone who crossed me. I was crazy enough to shoot anyone for anything. But no more. I want something better.

James: Jail changed my attitudes, too. So did turning to God. I'm still a member and I still believe in the Vice Lords, but I don't gang-bang anymore. I want to do more than that with my life. The only time I'm really tempted to get back in is when some friend of mine is hurt. Like not long ago when another gang killed my uncle because they mistakenly thought he was a Vice Lord. I got a gun and started to go out for revenge when something inside me said, "Don't go." So instead I stayed home and cried.

These days I tell my three little brothers to stay out of any organization. Gangs aren't worth it.

Joey: I was always proud to be a Dragon. After I'd been in for a while I realized how much money I could make dealing drugs and doing other things for the gang. What turned me around were a couple things. One, a girlfriend who didn't want to marry some criminal gang member. And two, turning my life over to God at a Bible study in the juvenile detention center.

My brother, a leader in the gang, sent someone over to beat me up when he heard I had become a Christian. But we worked it out and now he knows what I will and won't do.

David: When I was just five years old I was born again at my church; I asked Jesus into my heart. But now the Puerto Rican Stones are in my heart, too. I think they always will be.

Milton: I think lots of us pray to God. I know I do. Every morning when I wake up I pray and ask God to protect me. I never know when I might get shot.

Gregg: Where do you want to be five years from now?

Joey: I want to be living right here in my old neighborhood with my wife and my little girl. I'm going back to school now and hope to do something with computers.

David: I always wanted to be a doctor. I still do, but I don't know. In five years I guess I want to be a father.

Luis: I want to have a family, an apartment, a job, and be able to help younger Stones when they need help or advice.

James: I'm going back to school and then to college to study electronics.

Milton: I want to be right here on my street corner as a

PEER PRESSURE

P.R. Stone. I'm devoting my whole life to the Stones and every morning when I wake up I think about the five points the Stones stand for: love, trust, peace, freedom, and justice. That's what we want for ourselves and our neighborhood.

John Patrick: I've just finished my G.E.D. Now I want to go to college to study pre-law and eventually work as a juvenile parole officer. Maybe in four or five years I'll find peace of mind.

JOURNAL
entry☑

Gang Territory!

Inner-city gangs claim a certain territory, which outsiders enter at their own peril. But don't groups outside the inner city do something similar?

- Draw a blueprint-type picture of your school on the facing page and mark the place where different groups hang out with a sign or symbol. For example, use a basketball to mark where jocks hang out, or a musical note for the choir room. Be sure to write the name of your school in the blank and mark the date of your blueprint!

- When I enter the territory of another "gang," is there a "sign" I should give to be accepted? (For example, if you want the jocks to accept you when you enter the jocks' territory, how should you act?) _____

_____

_____

- What is the "sign" in your group? _____

_____

_____

_____ **HIGH SCHOOL**

Today's Date: _____

JOURNAL entry

Straight from the *Heart*

David said, "When I was five years old, I was born again at my church; I asked Jesus into my heart. But now the Puerto Rican Stones are in my heart, too. I think they always will be."

- Who are the most important people or groups living in your heart? *Write their names on the heart below.*

- Who is the leader in your heart? *Underline that name.*

- How can you tell?

Today's Date: _____

Problems
With
Cliques

The Unwritten Rules

Verne Becker

WHAT ARE YOUR SOCIAL HABITS?

You're in a locker-lined hallway. Nameless faces shove along in one great mass of humanity. You find yourself moving with them. It seems the thing to do—to move along, with the crowd.

You find that it's comfortable being caught up in the stream, in the rush and rumbling of others—but eventually you tire of moving with the crowd. It's so homogeneous. And so monotonous.

I spin the dial twice, stopping at fourteen. Twice in the opposite direction, stopping at twenty-seven. Then a quarter-turn to three. I pull on the handle and my locker door pops open. I fish for my history book beneath a mangled mass of papers, books, and two uneaten lunches in paper bags.

A roar of laughter in the background distracts me and I look to my right. About ten guys are standing in the hallway, five on each side, razzing people as they walk by. I pass them every morning, same time, same place. They are one of the school's foremost cliques—the rowdies.

PEER PRESSURE

I linger at my locker for a minute, thinking about other cliques I'll encounter during the day: the super athletes, with their girlfriends in tow; the burnouts, standing guard at the men's room; the artsy types, armed with Rapidograph pens; the journalism junkies; the rock 'n' rollers; and others. Each group sticks together like nuts in a Payday candy bar. Each has its own turf, its own entrance requirements, its own set of unwritten rules. Funny how easy it is to spot each group.

I kick my locker door shut and shuffle down the hall toward homeroom. As I mull over these unwritten rules, several scenes come to mind.

BACKFIRED

Sandy was excited. The impossible had just happened. Sue had called and invited her to a slumber party, and three or four of the most popular girls in school were coming. Sandy had wanted to get their attention ever since her family moved to the area last spring.

Friday night finally came. After eating pizza and playing piles of albums, the girls sat around on the floor of Sue's room in their pajamas, trying to think of good pranks to play on another girl at school who they were going to invite to another slumber party. Judging by the girls' squeals of laughter, Sandy kept coming up with the best ideas (like pouring hot sauce in the girl's mouth after she fell asleep). Laughter—it made her feel so accepted, so significant. Everyone finally collapsed into bed at about three in the morning.

The sound of a car starting in the driveway woke Sandy at 9:00 A.M. She felt a burning sensation in her mouth. Mexican hot sauce! Sitting up in bed, she looked around. The other girls were nowhere in sight. Neither was her suitcase or her clothes. Running to the window, she saw her

new friends pulling out of the driveway in Sue's green Toyota.

Tearfully Sandy realized what had happened. The girls had planned the whole party to be a setup. *She* was the girl for whom the pranks had been intended; she was the victim.

Unwritten Rule #1: Only hang around with other members of your group. Ridicule everyone else. Organize parties and other special events designed to exclude outsiders.

TRANSFORMATION

Though Christy was a simple, friendly, attractive girl, nobody really noticed her during her freshman year. At least, not the people that mattered. After all, she bought her jeans at Penney's, pulled her long brown hair into a ponytail, wore very little makeup, and liked classical music. But in the spring Christy made the cheerleading squad and after that she was never the same. All of a sudden the "right" people took note.

When school began in the fall, Christy had discarded her Penney's denims for Calvin's and turned in Beethoven for Springsteen. Sporting a fancy new hairstyle and an added supply of makeup, she fit right in with the other cheerleaders and never strayed far from them at school. Guys started asking her out, and she quickly joined the weekend party scene.

Now everyone liked Christy—at least the people who mattered did. The others just wondered where the simple, attractive Christy they knew had gone.

Unwritten Rule #2: Adopt the same habits, styles, interests, and attitudes as the rest of the group. Strive for absolute conformity.

WHO YOU KNOW

Sitting in the crowded bleachers for the first home football game was Bill Stockwell, basketball captain and most worshiped guy in the senior class. Bill had his own little following—sort of like servants—who escorted him between classes and sat with him at one of the center tables in the lunchroom. Several servants had joined him for the football game.

Late in the game Steve Barton sidled up to Bill and struck up a conversation. Over the din of the crowd and the blaring loudspeaker, one could hear a few of their words: "It was so funny, I was bombed out of my mind! Hey, did you make it home from Hanson's party last week?"

Bill just listened at first, but then responded with a few stories of his own and they both roared with laughter. Just as the game ended, a couple of other guys, along with Steve and Bill, squealed out of the parking lot in Bill's Mustang.

Monday during lunch hour the usual crowd gathered at Bill's table—but the group had gained a new member. There, along with Bill and his followers, sat Steve. His plan had worked.

Unwritten Rule #3: Acceptance by the group depends on whether you impress the unofficial leader.

COVER UP

Marilyn Schmidt earned the title "Stickwoman" during her sophomore year, mainly because she was 6'1" and weighed only 110 pounds. Kids cracked old jokes such as, "If she drank cherry soda, she'd look like a thermometer." Worst of all was second period P.E. class when she had to wear a gym suit. Marilyn became the target for everyone's ridicule.

Bradley Smith had an assigned seat next to Marilyn in English Comp. During the first weeks of the quarter he discovered that despite her bony elbows and knees, Marilyn had a pleasant personality. She wasn't a potential girlfriend, just a friendly person.

One day Bradley learned that Gary, a yearbook photographer who belonged to the group Bradley hung around with, had secretly snapped a photo of Marilyn in her gym suit. Gary wanted to hang several prints in the school halls for laughs. As Gary presented the idea to a few of the guys during homeroom, Bradley felt a knot in his stomach. He wanted to say, "C'mon, Gary—she's a nice kid, let's not hurt her feelings." But as the others laughed about how funny it would be, Bradley found himself laughing too. The photos appeared the following morning.

For some reason, Bradley felt awkward walking into English Comp class. Next to him sat Marilyn, wiping her eyes discreetly with a Kleenex. She looked up, but before her eyes could meet his Bradley turned his head and pretended to search for some papers.

Unwritten Rule #4: Don't reveal your true feelings about someone or something until you know what the rest of the group thinks. Follow whatever they say, whether you agree or not.

As I finish my musings, I decide I'm glad I'm not part of a clique. I make it to homeroom just as the bell rings, and quickly scan the faces of the people in the room. I spot several guys and girls who work with me on Student Council. I walk to the far side of the room and take a seat beside them.

JOURNAL
entry

Jesus dealt with peer pressure

... but he didn't reject anyone.

READ:

- **Matthew 4:1–11**
  Thought: Jesus wasn't pressured into doing what he knew was wrong.
  Application: What things do I give in to because of pressure from others?

- **Matthew 6:1–4**
  Thought: Jesus said not to do things just for show.
  Application: What do I do simply because I want others to see or notice me?

- **Matthew 7:1–5, 15–20**
  Thought: Jesus rejected outward show and stressed the importance of inner values.
  Application: What values are important to me, apart from fads, fashions, and looks? (For ideas, see 1 Corinthians 13 and Galatians 5:22.)

PEER PRESSURE

- Matthew 9:10–12; 11:19; Luke 19:1–9
  Thought: Jesus built friendships with society's outcasts.
  Application: Am I willing to make friends with someone who is not part of my group? If so, with whom?

Today's Date: _____

The Invisible Signs

Steve Lawhead

THE OUTSIDERS

What would happen if we suddenly decided to befriend someone outside of our group or clique? Would our old friends reject us? Would it be worth the risk? Steve says there's only one way to find out.

There is an invisible sign in the middle of the cafeteria. It reads: Territory of the Senior Class Socialites—All Others Keep Out! Although the sign is invisible, everyone can read it. Everyone knows and obeys. There are other posted territories: the far end of the student concourse, near the drinking fountain, the grassy hill in front of the school entrance. No trespassing! Keep out! This area belongs to us!

Belonging. That's what those invisible signs mean. To those on the inside they form the boundaries of a refuge, an island of safety in a sea of self-consciousness.

My group has staked out the lunchroom. From the security of our island in the middle of the lunchroom, I sometimes feel guilty as I look out at the loners. They sit alone, eat alone. Or they slouch unobtrusively behind their books and act like they're studying.

But they're not studying; they're watching us. Their eyes betray them. I've seen the looks of unguarded envy they

PEER PRESSURE

throw our way. They are saying, "If only I could join the group . . ." But it's impossible—there are unwritten rules governing these things.

I can only imagine what the outsiders are feeling. Yet some days there is a split second of uncertainty just before I reach my group. I wonder, *What if they don't recognize me? What if they don't let me in?* But I approach and the ranks open to admit me. I slap my tray down and I'm in—safe inside for another day.

I have learned to play the games you have to play to fit in. I know all the moves, the rules, the talk. I wear the mask the group wears and never, never let anyone see the real me. There's security there. I'm in, I belong. As long as I go along with the group—do as they do, act as they act, think as they think. Those are the rules. Break them and you're out. Then you'll be a loner holding your tray and looking for a place to sit. On the outside looking in.

I sometimes argue with the guilt: *Is it my fault for enjoying what everyone wants? What am I supposed to do? Quit? If I quit the group, what good would that do? Who would that help? Could I just walk away and be myself?* Deep inside I know the answers. Deep inside I must admit the truth: I *need* the clique. I'm too afraid to stand alone, to be myself. My fear keeps me tied to the group.

Still, I'm haunted by the eyes of the outsiders. They're always watching. I used to think they could tell I was different, that even though I ran with the group I still had my own identity. Now, I'm not so sure. Last week I saw a kid in the library—one of those who sits alone at lunch and studies while we're all cutting up. We were looking for the same book, he and I. We saw it the same instant and reached for it. I got there first. I looked at his eyes behind the thick glasses and felt a little sorry for him. I wanted to do a friendly thing so I offered the book to him. He looked at it, then at me, and turned his back. As he walked away, I heard him mumbling to himself. The others said the kid was a stuck-up snob when I told them. Funny, that's what he'd muttered about me.

Why do we have to have these cliques? Why can't we all just be ourselves? Unself-conscious. Not pretending to be the laughing, careless, and cool people we're not. I wonder, what is everyone afraid of? If I decided to take one lunch hour and sit with a loner, what would happen? What if we all did that? There'd be a revolution—a quiet revolution. And a lot of people would be freed that day. But I don't look for anything like that to happen. It's just too hard.

A choice must be made. I can see that now. It would be better if one or two of my friends in the group saw that, too. Maybe they do. Maybe they feel the same way I feel— trapped, stuck in the clique, but afraid to leave. Maybe they're waiting for someone to break free, to step out and risk something new.

There's one good way to find out.

SO ... FIND OUT!

Taking the risk to meet people outside of your group of friends doesn't need to be as scary as Steve makes it sound. There is a simpler way of going about it—a less frightening way than denouncing your group and throwing yourself into a friendless world. Here's how:

Over the next four or five days make contact with two people outside your regular groups of friends. Here are some tips to get you started:

Consider kids younger than you. They often want to get to know people in the grades above them.

Be sure your initial contact allows for a very short conversation. This will help take some of the risk and fear out of this exercise. Remember, these are just initial contacts. No life-long (even long-term) commitments here.

Here are some specific places and ways to meet someone for a short conversation:

PEER PRESSURE

In the lunchroom. As you stand in the cafeteria line, be sure you are the last person in your group. Then start a conversation with the person behind you. To break the ice, try to think of something you and this other person may have in common: "You're in my history class, aren't you?" If nothing else, talk about the weather or the lunch menu. Anything to get yourself going. Getting started is half the battle to meeting others outside your group. Then, before you grab your tray, take the next most important step—say, "By the way, my name is . . . What's yours?" Don't forget that name.

In class. You are bound to be sitting next to someone you don't know very well in at least one of your classes. Talk to this next-door stranger about last night's assignment, some TV show you watched, the concert you attended last weekend. Again, if you don't know the person's name, get it, and give that person yours.

At the bus stop. You can skim the books someone is carrying to think of something to say: "Oh, I see you have sophomore English. Do you have Simmons? I had him last year. He was a pain." Again, end the little chat by saying, "By the way, my name is . . . What's yours?"

In the parking lot. If you drive, park someplace different. Pull in beside someone who is also just pulling in. As you're getting out, comment on the person's car or the weather. Think of something that is happening today and use that to continue the conversation ("Are you going to the pep rally at noon?"). Walk into the school with this person, and continue to talk about things like morning classes or what you may have watched on TV last night.

The locker "next door." Do you know the person whose locker is next to yours? (Two lockers down? Across the hall?) You may know that person's name, but have you ever really talked to him or her? Make it a point to say more than hi. As this locker neighbor starts down the hall toward his or her class, walk along. Just say, "You know, we've had lockers next to each other and I don't even know what year you're in or what classes you're taking." Again, if you don't know the person's name, get it.

Gym class. After gym, while you're getting dressed, it would be easy to get into a conversation. Since people appreciate others noticing when they do something right, say something like: "You made that last goal didn't you?" It's important to pick up on some positive thing this person did during gym class—and talk about it. Again, find out that name.

Next, think of three new questions that dig a bit deeper than your first ones, questions you can ask this person when you see him or her again: "Where do you live?" "Are you into the Industrial Revolution in history class yet?" "Have you thought about going out for intramural sports next year?"

The next time you meet the person—in the hall, the parking lot, the lunchroom, by your locker—call him or her by name. This will show you care enough to remember who he or she is. Then ask at least one of the new questions you wrote down.

At this point you may have planted the seeds for a new friendship. At least you have proven to yourself that you can take the risk in breaking out of your safe group to meet new people.

What About Christians?

Jim Long

"CHRISTIAN" CLIQUES

So far we haven't said much about Christians. So what about 'em? Do they take some kind of anti-clique shot from the school nurse each September? Hardly. As a matter of fact, they have a tendency to cloister like monks in a medieval abbey—sheltering themselves from all worldly evil. Consider Jim's story.

The scene seems absurd now: standing with Janna on the sidewalk in front of her house, the two of us drenched to the skin. We'd been caught in a summer downpour and had run home, but then stopped—there in the rain—to talk. Janna's dark-brown hair hung in dripping curtains around her face, framing her striking, light-blue eyes. She was laughing.

We had first met at church a year earlier. She had appeared at a party with another girlfriend and had just kept coming back. Janna was never quite accepted into the group. Not that she was offensive or unattractive. Quite the opposite was true.

Perhaps she was cautious, afraid of becoming too religious. She did have a completely different circle of friends at school. The church kids never knew how to handle that. But then, neither did Janna.

She seemed to be reaching at times, trying to initiate a conversation that never got off the ground or going out of her way to welcome visitors. She even came to choir rehearsal (until the director kicked her out for laughing when the basses couldn't get their part).

Somehow she just didn't fit in. Maybe it was the religious thing. She was not a Christian. Her folks were not Christians. Her other friends were not Christians. And I'm not even sure she thought of me as a Christian—at least not in the way she thought of others.

She could not follow the strange terminology Christians used to describe their religious experience. The one time I had tried to tell her about Christianity she said, "You sound just like John" (an insult). John was constantly talking about Jesus but living just like everyone else.

As I looked at Janna—attractive, fun-loving, and *drenched*—I realized that one reason I found her so appealing was that she was different from most of the Christian girls I had known. She was unusually honest about her feelings and crazy enough to make life interesting.

Janna had chosen that rainy afternoon, on the sidewalk in front of her house, to tell me her dad was being transferred to Cleveland—a 2,500-mile move. We both cried and we both blamed the rain.

Since then I have often thought about Janna and wondered about her feelings, about what it was like to be on the outside—and I have come to a few answers and questions that seem sensible and fair.

1. Churchgoers often say they are citizens of another kingdom, the kingdom of heaven. But does that have to mean that anyone who is curious about the faith must spend a semester at some celestial language lab in the attic of a church trying to crack the code? "Born again."

TIGHT LITTLE CLIQUE, AREN'T THEY?

"Redeemed." "Christ in your heart." I realize it's natural that such an unusual, life-changing experience as becoming a Christian would involve a few new terms. But couldn't we have shared Christianity in terms Janna could understand? Couldn't we have just said it plainly?

"By setting forth the truth plainly, we commend ourselves to every man's conscience in the sight of God" (2 Corinthians 4:2).

2. Jesus told the story of a shepherd who had 99 of his 100 sheep safely corralled, and who went out looking for the one that was lost. But non-Christians sometimes feel Christians have locked the gate, loaded the shotgun with rock salt, and stand ready to blast away at the first strange sound. God expects Christians to value moral purity, but not to assume they are somehow superior to others. Can't Christians value goodness without becoming religious snobs? Couldn't we have maintained high standards and still have been a friend to Janna?

"If you think you are standing firm, be careful that you don't fall!" (1 Corinthians 10:12).

3. It used to be a standard cafeteria prank to stuff a piece of napkin into the lid of a saltshaker to frustrate unsuspecting fellow students. *Shake . . . shakeshake . . . shakeshakeshake.* Nothing.

Jesus said that Christians were to be the salt of the earth; they were to have a positive impact for him. It does not take much imagination to visualize a grain-of-salt Christian, peering at a plate of bland fries (outsiders) through the prospective glass of the saltshaker (a Christian in-group), thankful that the holes in the shaker are plugged.

Non-Christians shouldn't have to fight for Christian acceptance. It should come naturally, warmly. *Shake . . . shakeshake . . . shakeshakeshake.* It pours.

Couldn't we have shown Janna the friendship she needed?

"If you really keep the royal law found in Scripture, 'Love your neighbor as yourself,' you are doing right. But if you show favoritism, you sin and are convicted by the law as lawbreakers" (James 2:8–9).

Janna often crosses my mind. I recall her dark-brown hair and light-blue eyes, her pleasant disposition, her wacky sense of humor. But most vividly I recall an outsider, never quite accepted by the Christian group. And I wonder, *Why weren't we responsible enough to accept her and then show her plainly what Christianity is all about?* Perhaps we even could have turned her outside in.

Cliques: Going Deeper

Trapping Others Inside Labels

Philip Yancey

LABELS, LABELS, EVERYWHERE

So far we've taken a fairly surface look at cliques: We've ripped off the school roof and peered down inside; we've talked about partying and put-downs . . . but not much has been done to "get under the skin."

Now it's time to ask: What really are the long-term, heel-grinding effects of labels? Answer: Read on.

A writing assignment took me to Chicago's legendary Cook County Jail. I wandered through the steel and concrete maze, ignoring the heckling from prisoners who were as restless as caged tigers. The memory that still stands out sharpest is a bulletin board at the end of each cell block. There, guards post the photos and crimes of all the inmates in that cell block. Beside the photo of each glowering prisoner is stamped in large block letters: MURDERER, RAPIST, ARMED ROBBER, CHILD BEATER.

That label defines the prisoner. It follows him wherever he goes—in the cafeteria, the exercise yard, the visiting

PEER PRESSURE

lounge. To everyone else in the jail he is known by that one-word label. The label that elicits the most mockery and snide remarks from the other inmates is the word *homosexual*, which is painted in foot-high letters above the appropriate cell block.

As I walked out of Cook County Jail into sudden blinding sunlight, it struck me that prison labeling is really just a crude exaggeration of what those of us on the outside do every day. We slap labels on everyone we encounter. Think about it. Where have you heard such labels as jocks, heads, greasers, brownnosers, rah-rahs? The lists in some high schools grow long and colorful. You can hear other lists by walking past any playground—or visiting an old folks' home, for that matter.

Labels are shortcuts that allow us to dismiss the people they're attached to more easily. For example, one teacher in my high school became known as a "socialist." Suddenly no one listened to his opinions on U.S. politics anymore. "Of course he'd think that," was the common attitude, "he's just a socialist." His opinions were blocked out, invalidated by the label we had given him.

Some labels are more personal: fatty, klutz, gay, flirt. These kind often are applied with a laugh, but they can slash deep into a person's psyche. Have you ever heard a fat person open up and share what it's like to be labeled? He may fend off a dozen cruel comments a day, smiling good-naturedly at the ribbing . . . but inside he bleeds.

The long-term impact of labels is frightening. Often a person *becomes* his label, whether or not he was that way originally. *Psychology Today* reported a revealing experiment. The testers assigned a teacher to a classroom full of children telling the teacher in advance which ten in the class had the highest IQs. Sure enough, after three months of study their grades were highest, their attitudes the best. After the study was completed, however, the testers revealed an astounding fact: The ten names they had given the teacher were actually those of the children with the lowest IQs! But because the teacher had expected the best from them and had treated them with the most respect and attention, they had excelled. Given a new label, "smartest," they performed like it.

Labels often lie like that, and when we stamp them on people they often become trapped inside that lie. Call a person dishonest often enough and he'll begin to act it. Call someone a slum dweller or worthless and he'll believe it. Call a person an "easy make" sexually and he may become that.

Even if the label is partially true, it can box in a person in a cruel way. C. S. Lewis, a brilliant Christian author, recalled how constant taunts about his clumsiness in sports kept him depressed and lonely during most of his youth. He even hinted that those experiences contributed to keeping him away from God for years.

If you ask a person with a handicap what he would like more than anything else in the world, you'll invariably get an answer like this: "I want people to accept me as a person in spite of my handicap." If he is blind, you'll hear, "I don't want to be defined as a blind person; I want to be known as a person who happens to be blind." Don't stop at the label, he is saying. Look past it to the person inside, and respect him for who—not what—he is.

OPENING UP THE BOXES

What this person is asking sounds suspiciously like a command Jesus Christ gave his followers. To paraphrase Matthew 7:1, "Don't label, and then you won't be labeled." I think Jesus was striking out against the kinds of labels that limit people, that box them in.

In his life Jesus met with prostitutes, tax collectors, members of oppressed minorities, and rural fishermen. Yet he never opted for the easier, shortcut method of branding them with a label. Instead of focusing on what they *were—*

he knew they were discontent with that—he appealed to what they could be. And he asks us to do the same.

How do I stop the grinding process of labeling? I have come across a near-foolproof way of reminding myself how devastating labeling is. It is, simply, to consider what labels do to me.

Labeling starts a pessimistic, downward spiral in me. "I can't tell good jokes at parties" becomes "I'm no fun at parties" and then "People don't want me around." My friends who overeat soon find themselves saying, "I'm the kind of person who overeats" instead of "I overeat"—a subtle but terrible difference. Or, "I'm a person who smokes" becomes "I'm the kind of person who has to keep smoking." Once again, labels have become a shortcut to denying the possibility of change.

God responds in the same way to both my tendency to label others and my tendency to label myself. He stops my self-defeating spiral and challenges me, through himself, to explode the traps around me. The Bible is full of encouraging examples. Consider the apostle Paul—labeled "Chief Christian-Hater" of his day. After becoming a Christian himself, Paul led the way to bring together the two groups of people who most despised each other—the Jews and the Gentiles. And Paul isn't alone. The Bible tells story after story of people who had huge flaws, yet somehow discovered God could use them anyway.

In fact, God tells us what he sees when he looks at us, his followers: "Long ago, even before he made the world, God chose us to be his very own, through what Christ would do for us; he decided then to make us holy in his eyes, without a single fault—we who stand before him covered with his love. His unchanging plan has always been to adopt us into his own family by sending Jesus Christ to die for us. And he did this because he wanted to! . . . Moreover, because of what Christ has done we have become gifts to God that he delights in, for as part of God's sovereign plan we were

ARE YOU THE PEER, OR AM I?

PEER PRESSURE

chosen from the beginning to be his, and all things happen just as he decided long ago" (Ephesians 1:4–5, 11 LB).

A label is a powerful thing—like a steel cage it can trap a person for life. Believing in the possibility of change can help crack open the cage. Believing in what a person can become, not what he is, revolutionizes the way I look at my friends. Often I catch myself sliding lazily back toward labeling; "She always reacts like that; he's a liar—you can't trust him; he's just lazy. . . ."

When I'm tempted to label other people unfairly, I try to remember what such labels do to me. Then I recall God's viewpoint. That person is capable of becoming "a gift to God that he delights in"! Suddenly I realize that I have within me the power to move a person closer toward or further from that goal. When I meet someone new, I can either box him in by labeling him or free him up by looking for the person of worth inside. The choice is mine.

JOURNAL entry

LABELS .

The most commonly used labels at our school are ...

Today's Date: _____

PEER PRESSURE

JOURNAL entry

Think about the names you've been called

. . . and the labels people have applied to you. Then complete this sentence:

- "Being labeled makes me feel . . .

_____

_____

_____

_____

NOW, think of someone you've labeled. Rewrite your mini-essay, in the same words, but using his or her name:

- "Being labeled makes _____ feel . . .

_____

_____

_____

_____

Today's Date: _____

The Ugliest Kind of Exclusiveness

Tim Stafford

STEREOTYPES

They keep us "safe" in our own groups. They allow us to avoid those who are different. And they are capable of destroying a person's individual dignity and worth. Tim tells us how.

At Bullard High school an invitation to join the Key Club was like a gold plaque certifying you as a member of the in-crowd. If you wanted to be popular, as nearly everyone did, you had to get in. Not far into my sophomore year I realized that and began to plan how I could make it.

The theory of the club was this: On the basis of outstanding achievement, the leaders and potential leaders of the school were asked to join. The current members then voted whether or not to allow someone to join.

That's what the rules said. Actually, as I later found out, the club was a loosely organized clique with unwritten rules about who could be a member. They chose their friends. They were nearly all pleasant, attractive, above-average students whose parents had money. They all exuded

PEER PRESSURE

self-confidence, which is why some of them were class presidents and captains of the football team.

They had been born expecting to be the best. They always stepped forward while everyone else was busy feeling self-conscious. They always knew the right thing to say. They were the "right" kind of people.

I wasn't, but I didn't know that. I didn't know about those hidden qualifications. Because of my grades and my school activities, I expected that I might soon be asked to join. Instead, I was passed by. Others were asked who (I thought) weren't as eligible as I and some of my friends. At first I thought it was just an oversight, or that those chosen had qualities I couldn't see. But gradually I became aware that my achievements would never be enough to get me in. My parents weren't well-off, I didn't look right, I didn't have the right friends—I wasn't one of them.

As a senior I still wanted very badly to be asked to join the Key Club, but for a different reason. I dreamed of standing before the club and scalding them with scorn as I declined the offer. I actually rehearsed the speech to myself: The principal point was that I had no interest in joining their little clique.

I never got the invitation, so I never got to make my speech. My anger stayed with me. I didn't dislike the individual members: they were pleasant people who just naturally lived gracefully, and I envied them. But I hated the system they were part of—the clique that pretended to be the "best-qualified" people, whose membership could never be cracked by someone who didn't fit, no matter how good that person was.

WHAT JEWS ARE LIKE

Little stereotypes can have huge consequences. When I visited Toronto, I stayed with Kevin. I loved the city, particularly because it's so strongly ethnic. Kevin, his sister

Kathy, and I toured the Portuguese section. I could have sworn I had accidentally stumbled into Lisbon. Dark-complected men stood in groups talking Portuguese, and fish markets and vegetable stands crowded their way onto the sidewalks. Later we entered the Jewish section, and Kathy began explaining to me why Jews were often financially successful: "They don't mind going bankrupt."

She explained that they would start one business after another. When a business slowed or failed, they would bail out, leaving their creditors hanging, and do it without a trace of guilt. Sooner or later, by trial and error, they would hit on a business that succeeded. But they left many bad debts behind.

Since I had just met Kathy, I wasn't anxious to start an argument with her. But I had to say something. I told her I thought it was wrong to let a few experiences prejudice her against a whole group of people. I said I thought that we ought to take people one at a time and not lump them together and stick labels on them.

My friend Kevin broke in. "Oh, you don't understand. Kathy is not prejudiced against Jews. That's just the way they are." In a few minutes of discussion that followed he said that it was no wonder the German people had lashed out at the Jews during World War II because they had such a "stranglehold" on the economy.

I didn't continue the argument; it was getting nowhere. Instead I sat in the car while we toured Toronto and thought how innocent prejudice can seem. No one ever thinks he is prejudiced: "That's just the way those people are." I imagine that before World War II most Germans would have agreed with Kathy's description of Jews; they were willing to believe the stereotypes. They had no intention of killing millions because of the "stranglehold" they— women, children, and old people, too?—supposedly held on the economy.

I guess little stereotypes can have huge consequences.

PEER PRESSURE

SOUTHERN GIRL IN AUSTRIA

If you want to really get to know people, better leave your labels at home. As a college student I had the opportunity to go to a two-week conference in Austria. Students from all over Europe came to a beautiful castle in the Alps. I got acquainted right away with the other Americans there. One of them was a girl from South Carolina—very pretty, perfectly dressed, extremely feminine, polite. She had the most achingly sweet drawl I had ever heard.

I instantly checked her off as a Southern belle, even though I had never met one. She fit my stereotype. *Such women,* I thought, *are strictly for decoration: pretty but brainless.* Besides, sweetness wasn't my style.

I saw quite a bit of her during my stay there, but during our conversation I kept thinking of her as a Southern belle—a curiosity, but of no interest as a friend.

I must have screened out every other aspect of her, because I didn't wake up until she was almost ready to leave. Then it hit me: there was no evidence at all for my stereotype. It was particularly ridiculous to think of her as brainless. She was working on her master's degree in nursing and planning to teach at a college level. She had held her own in every discussion. She had never been insipidly sweet. If I hadn't been distracted by her accent, I might have really been interested in her.

It was no big deal. I have no idea whether a real friendship might have formed or not. I didn't bash my head against the wall when she left. But it did make me think. Had I missed out on an enjoyable relationship because of a stupid stereotype? And how many other potential friends had I passed by because I stuck them in a stereotype: jock, or cheerleader, or greaser?

I guess it just makes sense: If you want to really get to know people, better leave your labels at home.

THE BIGGER LIE

The world is full of cliques. Consider your school. The classifications usually are "stones," "jocks," "greasers." Some schools throw in "intellectuals," "science nuts," "politicans," "Bible thumpers." Some cliques don't have a name, but most people fit into one. Maybe it would be more accurate to say most people are put into one, whether they fit or not.

School is a small world. In the bigger world there are bigger cliques: black vs. white, business vs. ecology, union vs. management, upper class vs. welfare, "our kind" vs. outsiders, us vs. them. Nobody thinks of his group as a clique, at least not a discriminatory one. But when an outsider—someone who "just doesn't fit"—tries to get in, he's kept on the fringes until he gets the idea and goes away. Nobody tries to help him fit.

Cliques depend on stereotypes. Stereotypes have, of course, some truth behind them. But they have a bigger lie: If you fit a person into a category, you understand him.

Each person on earth is a totally unique creation. Thinking you understand someone because you know his category is like thinking you understand butterflies because you've seen one in a book. God has put a lesson in the life of every individual; there is part of God's personality stamped on each bit of humanity. You are going to miss that if you dismiss someone as a "doper," "jock," or "God-squader."

Not only that, but stereotypes are dangerous. They're cruel, as you know if you've ever been excluded. They feed the misunderstandings and hatreds that lead to war and discrimination.

I have a proposal: I would like to see closed little cliques open up, particularly to those who "don't fit." If there is something good holding your group together, you ought to want to share it. What holds most little groups together, however, is the "us vs. them" mentality. It's always ugly

PEER PRESSURE

(particularly when it's "us" Christians vs. "them" non-Christians). I can't think of anything finer than a person who sincerely tries to appreciate what is good in everyone he or she encounters. I can't think of a finer school than one where groups really get together, where there aren't barriers. It has to begin somewhere. Why not with us?

The Gamesman

Ralph Garza

ESCAPE: IS IT POSSIBLE?

Wondering if there's no escape from the clique trap? Well, don't lock yourself in your locker and throw away the combination. We're going to close this section on an upbeat note: Yes, there are "clique breakers"! In the following story, Ralph tells about some such people who changed his life.

School is a game—a big, mixed-up game made up of smaller games with hundreds of players, each one playing for himself. Winners are those who play games better than other people.

Consider the status game, "I'm his friend." The idea here is to make friends with the influential members of whatever group you think is the best. If you want to be on the yearbook staff, for example, you get chummy with the kids who are heading it up, get included in some of their activities, show them what a good guy you are. Friendship is a commodity you can sometimes use to good advantage. In high school, being in the elite is mostly a matter of who you know.

There's only one thing wrong with playing games: it eventually burns you out. I played the games thinking that

PEER PRESSURE

was what it took to be happy. But it wasn't working for me; I wasn't happy. Playing games was hard work, with incredible pressure. I could never relax and be myself because I was always afraid of what someone might think or say.

But I stuck in there like a master gamesman. I had a girlfriend—Linda—very cool, very "with it." She was part of an elite group at school, the one with all the popular and influential kids in it. Through my girlfriend, I had managed to become one of the regular members. Linda and I would show up at a party and everyone would wave, smile, and call out, "How you doing? Glad to see you." I was a guy to be envied—I could just imagine some of my old friends going green with jealousy when I walked in the door.

Then one night the roof started caving in. I don't know why, but Linda and I had an argument. She wanted to break up. We did, and suddenly I found myself on the outs with these people; they wouldn't have anything to do with me. The game I had been playing so carefully for so long was over—and I had lost. All my neat new friends mysteriously evaporated. When I walked down the hall at school there were no smiles or nods in my direction.

My nice little game was broken up, and that hurt. I struggled to get back in control as soon as possible, but I didn't have any way to do that. The tension built up inside and I couldn't release it (one of the rules of the game is that you never lose control). So I tried to hide it. But when I woke up in the morning the tension would start. My nerves began wearing thin and other people noticed I wasn't handling it too well. For someone who only wanted to be himself, to be happy, I spent a lot of time being miserable. I started looking around at the various groups in school to see what they had to offer.

The stoners were into dope, but that didn't make them happy, exactly—they were too afraid of being caught. Kickers were the redneck cowboy types who wore boots and hats and tooled leather belts with big buckles. They got their kicks by seeing who could get the drunkest. Some fun. The greasers were totally out to lunch with their street gangs, fighting all the time. It didn't take long for me to figure out that their game was much too dangerous.

That left just one other group—the Christians. In my school they were a small but conspicuous group. I'd gone out with girls who told me things like, "Jesus loves you, Ralph." But I didn't buy any of it. It was just part of their game. The first time someone asked me to go to a Campus Life club meeting, I didn't know what it was. I was surprised when it turned out to be a group of Christians getting together to talk about life and God.

I felt like leaving when I found out they were Christians, but I hovered in the background and waited until the meeting was over. I was surprised again when the meeting closed and there was no hard sell. I'd expected to have to fight my way out of there, but everyone was so nice to me I soon lost my fears of being "attacked" by those out to convert me. Jack, the club leader, also impressed me. I started thinking, *Maybe it's not a game, after all.*

I went back to Campus Life after that, and kept going back. I was at an all-time low in the friendship department, so the main thing I noticed was the friendship I saw displayed. It got to me. These people were interested in one another and it wasn't because they were playing games— they really cared. It was so different from the phony friendships I'd known before.

Amazingly, too, I felt no pressure. I could walk up to anyone and talk to him about anything. When you're playing the status game you can't do that. You have to play it cool and always be seen with the right people. For example, you go to a football game and you're looking for a place to sit. One of your friends yells out, "Hey, over here! Sit with us." But at the same time you see the other group you've been trying to crack—this is a good opportunity to get in with them. Now, if you sit with them, your other friends will feel snubbed and get down on you. If you pass up the opportunity, you'll look like you don't belong to the group. That puts a lot of pressure on you. These Christians weren't like that though. They were on a completely different wavelength.

I saw the difference most clearly in Jack, the club leader. To me, he represented a person who had it all under control: He was good-looking, well-liked, cool. He always knew the right things to say and do in any situation. He would have been a winner at any game he played—yet he depended on God. *If a guy like Jack needs God,* I reasoned, *then there's no doubt that I do, too.*

I reached a point where I had to make a choice: say yes to Christ or forget the whole thing and look elsewhere. It came down to that. There was no big emotional struggle. In fact, there was no struggle at all, really. I just saw very clearly what I had to do. The Christians as a group offered all the things I was looking for. With them I had friends who cared about me, without the games where I had to impress people or put on a fake front, and without pressure. I went with the Campus Life group for a ski weekend and accepted Christ there. I've been growing ever since.

Sometimes I wonder why I didn't think of God sooner. I knew about him, because my parents are Christians. The games I played were so shallow and unsatisfying—why did I play them for so long? My only excuse is that, from the outside, Christians looked just like any other cliquey group.

Then, when I bothered to look at them closer, I saw it wasn't a game at all. That's when I learned something most people are never willing to admit: You play games because you're not comfortable with who you are; you're not free to be yourself. Christianity is different because it frees people just to be themselves. When there's no pressure to be something you're not, all kinds of good things can happen.

Christ is real, and he frees his people to be real, too. That's not a game.

JOURNAL
entry✓

Is Christianity a Clique?

- List four people you're pretty sure aren't Christians—or at least aren't in a Christian group:

  1. _____

  2. _____

  3. _____

  4. _____

- List four ways you can invite one (or all) of these people to experience your Christian group:

  1. _____

  2. _____

  3. _____

  4. _____

Today's Date: _____

Using Peer Pressure

Sandbagger

Barbara Durkin

YOU DON'T HAVE TO BE SUPERMAN

So far so bad.

Peer pressure. It looks like an insurmountable power. Like a 300-pound football tackle plowing everybody over.

But imagine this: You, facing "Brute Force" head on—all 110 pounds of you—and stopping him. Impossible? Not on your life. This book was written because it *can* be done. By you. You can turn peer pressure back on itself. You can use peer pressure—good peer pressure—to do good things.

Take Gene and his buddy, Joel, in the following fiction story.

Once, when I got food poisoning at a Boy Scout picnic, I felt so rotten I thought I'd die. Rotten isn't even the word for it. I believed then that nothing could ever match that feeling of low-down wretchedness.

I was wrong.

This morning I recalled that feeling, and just like the first time, I thought I might die.

I'm more of an Indian than a chief: I'm a follower who would rather let cooler heads prevail. I prefer to do my little

PEER PRESSURE

part in any given project and be done with it. Let the movers and the shakers do the worrying and planning. Let them take all the credit, and all the blame, too, if things fall apart.

"You know what we used to call guys like you in college?" my dad asked me once. "We called 'em 'sandbaggers.'" Everybody else was hustling, all eager and panicky, and then there'd be some character like you, Gene—some guy who just piddled and potzed and did the absolute minimum, and then somehow managed to pass all the quizzes and squeak through the exams with gentlemanly grades. That's you, Gene. Effort, 2; Achievement, 7. It's not fair, son—not to you, nor the people who are trying to guide you."

"I'm okay, Dad," I said. I always say that to him. He's a great guy, but he never really takes it easy. Doesn't know how, I guess. He's a born chief, and he takes things very seriously. Like our soccer team. Dad's been an assistant coach for a long time, but it frustrates him to no end that some of us aren't hotshots out there on the field.

"I don't get it!" he yelled at me once. His face was scarlet, his shirt soaked with perspiration behind the bright whistle. I was dry as a bone and that had gotten to him, I think.

"Why play at all if you're not playing your best? Why bother if you don't play to win?"

"Because it's still fun, Dad," I told him. "It's still fun just being out there on the field, helping out a little. I just don't care about being a star, okay? I'm not an outstanding player, and that's all there is to it."

"Maybe not," Dad said. "But the thing you don't understand is that one of these days you just might be called on to do something extraordinary, and you've got to be ready. The way things are going with you, I'm afraid you won't be."

I wanted to say something funny and offhand, but

nothing came to me. Finally I said, "I get it, Dad," and hoped he was satisfied.

All he said was, "Good, Gene."

That was last summer, when I was a month short of seventeen, so I guess he figured if I hadn't made any major changes in attitude by then, it was pointless to keep harping on the subject. Besides, he could always count on Mom to take up where he left off.

"These grades are hardly a reflection of your abilities," she said a few weeks ago. She took off her violet-tinted glasses and looked right through me, tapping her perfect nails on the Formica top of our kitchen table. My report card lay out in front of us, and I could hear my sister Alicia glowing and humming behind me. Alicia is a high achiever who's always been placed in the G/T (Gifted/Talented) program. In fact, everyone in our family is G/T except me. Even Duffy, our sheepdog, aced doggie obedience school and now does everything except cook and cut grass.

"It's disappointing, Gene," she said. She fluffed up my hair the way she did when I was a little kid. I don't mind when she does that, though. It makes me realize that my laid-back posture hasn't alienated us.

"It's disappointing because you and I both know you could do much better. You could do great things if you'd only take yourself seriously."

"What's wrong with just doing good things? Why does everybody have to be exceptional in this family? Isn't it enough for you that Alicia is Little Miz Perfect? Can't you bask in her glory and leave me out of it?"

"You're not getting the point, Gene," she said tiredly, sadly. "This isn't a contest between you and your sister—or you and anyone else, either. We only want you to look yourself squarely in the eye, Son, and know you've done your best. So far you haven't done that, and you're nearly eighteen."

"Yes, I have," I said. "I know myself very well, and I

PEER PRESSURE

realize that I'm just sort of a sandbagger, like Dad says. But I like it. It suits me. Is that so bad, really? Aren't you still nuts about me, even with all my faults?"

"Yeah," she said and squeezed my hand. Then it was time to think of Christmas and everyone left me to my own devices again. That is the way I've always liked it—no pressure.

Joel Blakemore is my best friend. He's somewhat hyper, but we get along perfectly. He goads me into accepting minor challenges, and I hang onto his skinny ankles when he tries to leap off mountaintops without a parachute. I also happen to think he's the funniest person I've ever met, and he thinks the same of me, so we're even. Together, we're just two happy loons minding our own business, the Scarecrow and the Tin Man dancing along toward Oz.

But we haven't been laughing too much lately.

This friend of ours from school, Kevin Tallegsen, just got his license before Christmas. He was out showing off a little, the way anybody would. He went to the Eastgate Village Mall to return some Christmas stuff, and he had his sister Vicki and her girlfriend Suzanne, a girl he was trying to impress, along with him. While they were inside, a light snow started to fall, and by the time they came out, the parking lot was pretty glassy.

You never know exactly what went on in a situation unless you were right there, I guess. I'm telling you what Vicki told Alicia and me, and so be it.

As they were leaving the mall, some kids came out of the movie theater after the 7:00 show. One of the kids zig-zagging around the slippery parking lot pavement was Richie Long, the thirteen-year-old brother of Roy Long, our school's all-conference football star. Kevin and Richie knew each other because they live on the same street, so Kevin offered him a ride home.

Richie turned him down, making some smart-alecky

remark about Kevin's driving. Then, with his junior-high buddies hooting and cheering, Richie started showing off like crazy by dancing around in front of the car and smacking the hood. Kevin started to pull away, but Richie jumped in front of the car and said something else about Kevin's driving.

"Cut it out, you little brat!" Kevin shouted, and that made Richie mad and twice as determined to act moronic. He started break dancing in front of the car, first moon walking across Kevin's path, then going down into a spin on his butt.

The kids were laughing at Kevin and clapping for Richie when Kevin threw the car into reverse and went slipping and sliding backward in the slush. Once Kevin had some room, he shifted back into drive and cut the wheel to the left to head off across the parking lot, away from Richie and his friends. But as Kevin accelerated, Richie came running at him as if he was going to leap up onto the hood of the car. Kevin panicked. Whether he hit the gas or brakes doesn't matter, because the car slid on the slippery pavement and hit Richie, sending him flying into the air and down onto his head.

His neck broke. He died before the paramedics got there.

It was on the news that night, and then of course there were all kinds of phone calls. The next morning Mom said I could drive over to Joel's, since he lived right around the corner from the Tallegsens and the Longs. When we got there, I was shocked to see how bad Joel looked.

"It was a rough night," he said, pushing at his glasses the way he always did when he was nervous. "My dad and some of the other guys in the neighborhood had to go running out into the cold to keep Richie's father from trying to shoot Kevin with his hunting rifle. After they got Mr. Long calmed down and Kevin had come home in the police car, nobody noticed Roy Long waiting near the sidewalk.

When Kevin got out of the car, Roy jumped him and messed up his face and was trying to bash his skull into the pavement. The police finally pulled Roy off and sent him home, but he was threatening Kevin the whole time."

According to Joel, Roy thought Kevin had been hot-dogging, and that the accident was really his fault. "You're gonna pay for this. You killed my little brother, and you're gonna be sorry. I'm gonna get you, Tallegsen."

Kevin's nose was bloody, and both eyes were black, but most of all he was in some sort of shock, Joel said.

Joel was looking pretty bad himself.

"Hey, take it easy," I said. "Be grateful it wasn't you."

"We've known Kevin for a long time," Joel said. "He's a decent guy and he doesn't deserve this. That much I know."

"You don't even know the full story yet, and you're all bent out of shape over Kevin. It's Roy and his family I feel sorry for. They're the ones who are really hurting," I said.

Joel just stared at me for a minute as if I were some bug-eyed alien he'd never laid eyes on before. Then he said, "Grow up, Gene," and before I knew it, I stood shivering out on his front porch, alone and bewildered. I went home mad, really mad at Joel for the first time in years.

For the next few days thousands of different versions of the accident were flying around, most of them melodramatic and only partially true. Finally it started getting to us all, even Alicia.

"This is sick," she said. "All Roy's friends have sworn they're going to make Kevin pay for what they think he did to Richie. It's so stupid. I can't understand how people can act that way. Don't they even care about the truth?"

When school resumed after Christmas break I believed that everyone would be sane again soon enough. Then, too, I didn't believe that the kids we knew, horsed around with, rode the bus with, and flicked towels in the locker room with would be capable of sustaining such a pointless vendetta against Kevin Tallegsen. That was movie stuff, soap opera stuff. This was the real world, our world, and we were safe from such made-for-TV nonsense.

But lots of people wouldn't let go of it. Kevin looked shaky and pale when he managed to get himself to school. He no longer went carousing through the showers and locker room doing bird calls and Springsteen imitations.

"He's kind of subdued, isn't he?" I said to Joel after about two weeks.

"Yeah, well, figure it out," Joel said. "Put yourself behind the wheel of his car that night. Then tell me you still feel like doing your Three Stooges routine."

"Okay, okay," I said. "I get the picture."

About that time the papers ran a series of stories about young drivers, and how dangerous a breed they are, careening around drugged or boozed up—accidents eager to happen. Now that made me mad.

"Thanks a lot, Kevin," I said aloud when I finished reading the article Joel had handed me. He and I were staying after school, sitting in the yearbook office cutting and pasting. At my reaction, Joel suddenly got up and took his lanky body elsewhere. Then he looked back across the cluttered office at me.

"I mean it, Gene," he said. "Quit adding to Kevin's problems. I'm serious."

"I'm not doing anything to Kevin," I said. "Boy, are you hard to talk to lately. Is it my breath?"

"Yes," Joel said. He could always make me laugh, no matter what the situation. I grinned. But he ended up scooping up all his loose papers and moving even farther away from me to finish his work. I felt like an idiot sitting all alone. I mean, I got my work done anyway, but it wasn't much fun alone.

Then it was February, the Valentine's dance was coming, and I started thinking about asking Suzanne. Vicki Tallegsen came over to visit Alicia after school one day about

PEER PRESSURE

that time, and since she knew Suzanne, I figured she'd know what my chances were.

But the instant I said, "I'm thinkin' about asking Suzanne to the Valentine's dance. Do you think she—," both Vicki and Alicia went out of order.

"How could you?" Vicki cried. "You know Kevin's still crazy about her. How could you do this to him?"

Funny, I hadn't thought of it as doing something to him, only of doing something nice for me. I figured they were overreacting and decided to call Suzanne right then. In the end, it turned out to be what my dad calls a "moot point," though. Suzanne turned me down with stunning alacrity. I walked back, disgruntled, to the family room to report the results.

"There, see? It didn't change the course of human events for me to ask her. Now Kevin can ask her himself if he wants to."

"Yeah, but he won't," Alicia said. "He doesn't dare. It might ruin Suzanne's life. See, anybody Kevin talks to gets into trouble with the Goon Squad."

"You mean those guys are serious about getting Kevin?"

"Grow up, Gene," Vicki said, her face crumpling now. "Where are you, anyway? Are you blind and deaf? Can't you see that nobody associates with Kev and me? Don't you see all those ugly little notes they tape to our lockers? People keep threatening to run over us and kill us in cold blood, like they think Kevin did to Richie. I'm scared to death, and Kev has me so worried. He wants to . . . wants to . . ."

"Leave, I bet, and I don't blame him," I said. Anybody would want to run away and hide after something like this.

"He wants to kill himself!" Vicki blurted. My stomach took a deep dip.

"Is he serious?" I asked.

"I think so. He gave me some of his favorite records, and he keeps talking about how much easier my life would be if he were out of the picture for good. I'm so scared." She was crying hard into the wad of tissues she clutched in her small hands. I wanted to put something around her—a warm quilt, or both my arms—to enfold her in security, but Alicia led Vicki away to her bedroom while I just stood there with both arms dangling. That was all right, though; Alicia could probably take better care of her than I could.

I walked over to Joel's, although the temperature was a bone-chilling 15 degrees or so above zero. He was lying on his back in his rumpled bed, arms behind his head, looking at his ceiling. He always referred to the ever-present, ever-shifting piles of books, papers, and other junk as "generic debris," and I carefully stepped through it as if I were sneaking through a mine field. Joel didn't like footprints on any of his precious paper scraps.

"Hey, Bones!" I said, putting out my foot to rouse him. "The man is here! Rise and shine. Daylight in the swamp!"

"Shh," he said. "I'm in a delicate condition. Don't jounce me around too much." He meant that he was thinking. You don't hang out with a guy as long as I had with Joel and not know what he means. I settled back and started to talk.

"Hey, it's too bad about Kevin and Vicki, huh? Vicki says life's hardly worth living for either of them now, especially at school."

"I don't know how Kevin puts up with all the grief he gets at school."

"Well, Vicki says he's half crazy. She says she can't get through to him anymore. He doesn't even want to go on living."

"How would you feel if you were in his shoes?" Joel asked me.

The thought chilled me, and I had to stop talking. Joel and I practiced tossing paper wads into his trash can backward, but my heart wasn't in it, so I went home just after nine.

PEER PRESSURE

The night was clear and almost silent as I trudged across town under the glowing streetlights. I wondered if the time would ever come for me when life would seem hopeless. It was colder than I'd thought it was. I pulled my coat up higher around my ears and walked faster. And I wondered if I'd ever feel as alone as Kevin must feel. As the chill seemed to seep into my bone marrow, I remembered stories I'd heard about people getting so cold that they stumbled senseless into snowbanks and just lay there until they died, all alone, thinking they were only resting for a while.

I ran the rest of the way home.

"Mom! Dad!" I called out as I flung open the door and stood panting in the mudroom. "I'm home!" I shouted through stiff lips.

"Good," Mom said sleepily from upstairs. "Okay, Son," Dad called up from the basement. For the briefest instant, I wished one of them had been right there with me, rather than separated from me by walls and stairs. And years. I went to bed shivering, and it wasn't until I'd said some heartfelt prayers for Kevin that I got warm enough to fall asleep at last.

This morning I was hanging out at the school store waiting for this gorgeous girl, Ellen, to come by so I could walk her to her class and ask her to the Valentine's dance. Kevin happened to come up, and he mumbled something to the redheaded girl at the counter.

"Please go away," she said in a near whisper. "I can't wait on you."

Kevin repeated his request. The girl just stood and stared at him without making a move to get the ballpoint pen he'd clearly asked for. He stood there looking awkward, and then his face went from pale to hot scarlet as she turned her back on him.

"What's the problem?" I asked casually. "Why don't you

get him the pen he wants? You have a whole box of them right behind you. Look."

She turned back around to face me, but she wouldn't respond at all. Her mouth was set like a baked pie crust, and she refused to come undone as I went on asking her to wait on Kevin. Then, out of nowhere, Joel showed up, and all three of us stood there.

A crowd quickly gathered—somehow people always seem to sense when trouble is coming. There was kind of a terrible calm all around us, and that's when I first started feeling ill, the way I did with the food poisoning.

Just then a troop of jocks came thundering down the hall like stampeding buffalo.

Why me? I thought as the horde swerved and re-grouped. *Why now?* I wasn't ready for all this.

"What's the problem, Terri?" one of the bigger guys rumbled in a voice that came from somewhere near the center of his considerable bulk.

"He wants to buy something," the girl muttered, looking down at the counter. "A pen."

"What's our policy on that?" the guy asked her.

"No sale, you told me," Terri replied.

"And why?"

"Because, because he . . ."

"Go ahead and say it. No, wait. I will." The hulking beast turned to face Kevin, who looked, suddenly, very thin and insubstantial. I could feel Joel beside me trembling, the vibrations jarring my elbow.

"It's because he murders little kids in cold blood," the guy said, stabbing Kevin with his eyes. "Isn't that right, Tallegsen?" Kevin just stood silently, his arms at his sides, like a condemned prisoner on his way to the chair.

Then I heard a familiar voice speaking.

"All right, that's enough of this nonsense." It was Joel's voice, unnaturally loud and very authoritative. Everyone was stone silent and Joel went crashing ahead.

PEER PRESSURE

"There's been enough damage done to enough people already. Just move on now, and find another axe to grind, okay? And tell your friends to lay off, too." He turned his back on the guy and spoke directly to Kevin.

"You're not alone here, man," he said. "I should have said this to you a lot sooner, but I didn't think . . . I mean, I didn't realize a lot of things before today. Don't let these guys get to you. You've always had friends here, and you still do."

"Oh, yeah?" Goliath said, butting in. He yanked Joel away from Kevin by the shoulder, sending Joel's books to the floor. "You and who else?"

Joel was standing tall, his thin arms and legs still trembling, his eyes bright with conviction. That sick feeling surged up inside me, and I thought I was going to be overtly ill.

"Me," I said. I used Joel's tactics, talking loudly to cover the panic I felt. I laid down my books and tensed for the inevitable carnage.

"Me, too," said the girl behind the counter. "I'm sick of you guys and your stupid games. Who do you think you are, kicking a guy like Kevin when he's obviously too screwed up inside to defend himself?" Her blue-green eyes were fiery, and now anger was overcoming her fear.

I was starting to feel better. Other voices were agreeing with us. Dozens of voices. And the big guy was getting confused, looking around him for the buddies who were fading into the background.

"Aw, you people are too stupid to bother with," the guy said when he realized at last that he was alone. He ducked away and disappeared.

"Hey, Kevin, good to have you back," I said, trying to fill up the awkward moment.

"Thanks," he said. "Thanks, you guys. Everyone. I . . . I don't know what to say. I . . ."

"Forget it," Joel said. He bent to pick up his books.

"Come and eat lunch with Gene and me, if it doesn't embarrass you too much. We don't call Gene 'Hoover' for nothing."

Kevin tried to smile. "Later," he said.

Now I know it's not the kind of thing you dash home to tell Mom and Dad about, like getting an A in American History class or something. But it was a big deal to me, and a very big day. I know the time will come when I might talk about the way I felt today—before the confrontation and now, afterward—with somebody special. A wife, maybe. Or a kid I might have someday. But for now, it's only important that I'm starting to see what I'm made of. Maybe I'm not that half-toasted marshmallow I've always thought I was. Maybe there's more inside me than I suspected.

JOURNAL
entry

Is Somebody Getting Dumped On?

- Does a group of seniors continually pick on a freshman or underclassman? Who?

- Is somebody rejected—even teased—because of race or ethnic background? Name him or her.

- Do "smart kids" call somebody dumb? Who?

- Is somebody the subject of gossip? Go ahead, name them—all of them.

    If I wanted to help, I could . . .

    1. _____

    2. _____

    3. _____

(Examples: Invite the person to a meeting you usually attend—such as your church youth group. Step in on the person's behalf when people are laying into him. Invite the person to join your group at lunch.)

Today's Date: _____

Making Changes

Steve Unwell, Doug Bannell, Lisa Hutchcraft as told to Chris Lutes

POSITIVES OUT OF NEGATIVES

Does anybody really turn negative peer pressure around? Most of us don't think about it much. We just stuff our hands into our pockets, shrug our shoulders, and let the negative stuff get to us. The bad often looks too overwhelming to conquer.

This story looks at several people who did, in different ways, take on negative peer pressure and win.

Steve: "I know it's important to expand my borders."

When I first became a Christian in high school, I really appreciated the fact that I was accepted for who I was—there seemed to be no strings attached. Yet as time went on I realized that even Christians have their own tendency to form cliques. We often form safe little groups, avoiding others who don't fit in.

That's the way it was with "Bill." Some of my friends would see him coming and do their best to get out of his way. I have to admit, there are a lot of things going against

PEER PRESSURE

him. The fact that he's somewhat of a slob is accentuated by a weight problem. He also has had a drug and alcohol problem—along with various medical problems. All in all, Bill is pretty much of a mess. But what really turns people off is that he can make a homecoming parade look like a funeral march. He is always down, always depressed. And this, paradoxically, has made him the laughing stock of the kids at school—including the Christian kids.

But I like Bill. While I know he can be a pain, I see him as a guy who has a lot of good qualities. He's a gentle, caring person. In fact, he is one of the nicest guys in the world if you give him a chance. Yet even though I expressed this to my friends, it didn't seem to make any difference.

Some, of course, have done what may be called their "Christian duty." They'll spend an hour with Bill, then not talk to him for maybe a month. Because of this, Bill feels betrayed. He's smart enough to know the difference between real friendship and just putting in "friendly" time.

Once, Bill came to the lunch table and started carrying on about his most recent problem. He had just gotten kicked out of his house and was on the verge of getting kicked out of school. He was talking about suicide and stuff like that. One of my friends interrupted him in the middle of his Hamlet-type soliloquy: "Bill, I'm sick and tired of you always being depressed." And with that, he got up and walked out.

I got really mad at this guy, so later on I confronted him. I asked him how he would feel if he were having a hard time and someone brushed him off like that. Somewhat to my surprise, he talked to Bill and apologized.

I'd like to think that along with helping Bill, being his friend, I have also helped others understand him better. True, it takes discipline to relate to a guy like Bill—to bring him into your circle of friends. It also takes a certain amount of risk. You may lose a friend here or there, but those kinds of friends were never really true friends in the

Wally Bodnik experiences a severe fad identity crisis.

PEER PRESSURE

first place. Since I've taken the time to get to know Bill, I think he's a really great friend. And not only has Bill gained from my friendship, but I have gained from his, also. He'd do anything for me, and I know that for certain.

Doug: "Keeping in sync."

Here at college I'm part of "crew," the sport where a crew uses short oars to row a long, narrow boat. In this sport it is essential that all the guys be in sync. If our actions aren't synchronized, we'll work against each other and get nowhere. So our team is only as good as the individual parts. If someone is lagging behind or not quite in sync, we work to build him up—to make him a better part of the team.

I use this analogy because it says a lot about a situation that came up with my group of friends. A couple of the girls got "out of sync" with each other. If the situation didn't change, we were going to lose something far more important than any contest: our friendships.

These girls room together and had always been very close. But suddenly one of the girls, I'll call her "Cindy," started giving "Pattie" a real hard time. Cindy, for no apparent reason, would say things to put Pattie down. For instance, Pattie had a slight cold and was coughing quite a bit. Cindy snapped at her, "I've been feeling a little sick, too. Don't think you're anything special!"

This may seem like a minor thing, but it went on all the time. I think they were terribly close to destroying a good friendship. They certainly were causing a lot of tension with my whole group of friends. On several occasions Pattie came to me in tears. While I am one to avoid any kind of confrontation, I felt something needed to be done. I decided to talk to Cindy about it—in private. Talking it out in the group would only have made her feel like everybody was ganging up on her.

When I finally approached her, she was a bit defensive. She didn't realize she'd been so negative. But the more we talked, the more she recognized the problem. I agreed with Cindy to mention it if she started getting hard on Pattie again. I also knew that Cindy didn't need rejection, she needed my friendship more than ever.

I can't stress how hard this was to do—to confront Cindy. And I can't stress how important it is to be very sensitive and loving when talking to someone about a problem like this. If you're not, it can backfire in your face. But if you just ignore it, the problem won't go away—it will only get worse.

I guess being a good friend means caring enough to stop a negative thing that's happening in your group. To get back to the rowing analogy, it's like getting the oars back in sync. When they're out of sync you get nowhere. When they're in sync the boat goes smoothly on course. And that's just like good friendships.

Lisa: "I like the challenge."

I'm the kind of person who looks at building friendships as a kind of challenge. But it's a fun challenge, especially if you know just a few "tricks of the trade." Here are a few I have used.

1. *Just a smile.* When I started high school as a freshman, I saw a lot of sour faces in the hallway. It seemed like nobody was happy; nobody smiled. Everybody was a stranger and appeared determined to stay that way. I decided to do something about it: I would smile and say hi to kids in the hall until others started smiling and saying hi back. For days it seemed like nobody noticed. If they did, they would simply look away. It was rather depressing. But each day after school I would go home and say to my mom, "I won't give up until somebody smiles back." In time one kid smiled, another said hi. And before long, I saw expressions change on some people's faces. Other kids took the initiative and smiled without being smiled at. I know it's just a little thing, but I'm still friends with some of the kids I met

through a hi and a smile. This is something I think anybody can do to break the ice.

2. *Clique-ing out.* So what about when you finally find that special group of friends? That's great, so long as that special group doesn't become so "special" that it excludes others. I know that some of my friends work hard at edging certain people out, and are quite successful. For instance, there's Mike. He's tall and skinny, has a really big head, and wears glasses. And he has a stuttering problem. Some of my friends see him and say, "Oh, my gosh, what a nerd; what a geek."

Instead of joining in on the put-downs, I try to take the opposite approach by doing certain little things to say I care. For instance, I try to remember people like Mike with a card at Christmas and on birthdays. Last Christmas I not only sent him a card, but he also sent me one. So we can help others give, too.

At Christmas a lot of the popular kids in our school send carnations to each other. There's a great deal of status in the number of carnations you get. When I first saw kids giving carnations to each other, I looked around and saw that a lot of my friends were being left out. I thought about how lonely those people must feel. So now I spend a little extra money buying some of these kids flowers during this time.

3. *Discover what's important.* Some kids spend a lot of time putting others down or talking about the stuff that can be destructive to a group and friendships. Instead, I think that one way we can build good friends and good groups is through remembering some little detail about each person we are close to and using it positively.

For instance, did you ever get introduced to someone and the next time you saw her she remembered your name? How did that make you feel? When I remember the little things, I show I really care about a relationship. Just saying "Is your mom out of the hospital yet?" demonstrates that I remembered an important detail about someone. And that makes that person feel important. It makes him or her realize I care.

My friend Sharon is a dancer. I'm not that interested in dancing, but it's something important to her. So I go to some of her competitions. One of my other friends is a singer, so I have gone to hear him sing. Another of my friends is a writer. He's a real nonconformist and some of his poetry is really unusual, but I care enough about him to ask about—and read—his latest writings.

I also think that when we pick up on the little things, we leave ourselves open for our friends to trust us with the bigger things. And knowing about these deeper problems helps us understand each other better. That is, we understand that a person isn't simply acting strange or weird for no reason at all.

One of my friends has gone through two divorces in her family. Most of the kids at school don't know that. They only know that she's very possessive. She hangs on to a relationship like another one is never going to come along. Because of this, they say harmful things about her. But I've taken the time to get to know her, and she feels free to talk with me, so I know the underlying reason for her behavior. And knowing that, I am not so tempted to reject her.

4. *It's party time!* My friends have always tried to get me to go to parties where there would be drinking or drugs. I don't care to go to those parties because, first of all, I don't drink, and secondly, I don't want to see my friends drunk.

Last year one of my friends planned this really big party and I was invited. I told him I didn't care to go, but I did want to show I cared about him. So I made some chocolate-chip cookies for the partyers and took them over early. When I handed them to the guy giving the party I said, "Well, when you've had too much to drink, have some of these." I know they drank a lot that night, but I wanted to show that I didn't reject them even though I didn't attend the party.

PEER PRESSURE

I think many of my friends are at these parties because there seems to be nothing else to do. When they are not being entertained with positive things they'll think of their own things to do. And a lot of times this means experimenting with stuff that's not so good.

I believe there are more fun, creative ways to have a party than simply getting loaded, having sex in the upstairs bedrooms, or taking drugs in the basement. This is where some creative alternatives to the current party scene come in. For example, for some time now my parents have thrown theme parties for my birthday. A theme party is a party where you center the party around a theme, like a Hawaiian luau or a popular movie like *Pretty in Pink*. After choosing the theme, you make a lot of "props" relating to the theme to put around the house. And, to make these parties work, they must be fast-paced, with a lot of different things to do.

My most recent party was called "A Teddy Bear Picnic." I know that may sound a little dumb to some of you, but all kinds of people showed up—and with their own teddy bears from their childhoods (that was one of the "requirements" for coming). Everybody seemed to have a great time. One of my friends who came was a real tough-guy type, a real drinker and partyer. But there he was, having a good time, with his old beat-up teddy bear under his arm.

Of course, parties like this take a lot of work. My mother had put a line of luminaries (lighted candles in homemade holders) on both sides of the driveway. There was a big teddy bear at the front door to greet everyone. The garage was converted into a big bear den, and we watched a Paddington Bear movie and played word games that had questions like, "What's intolerable?" (Answer: un*bear*able.) Yet despite the work it takes to put such parties on, they're well worth it.

And what's really neat is that they catch on.

Several friends have come to me and asked, "Can you help me plan my party?" They get so sick of the regular party garbage that they want something different, something more creative. This is what happened with Jenny, a girl in my class.

Jenny came to me after my most recent birthday party and said, "Lisa, I want to have a really good party." While Jenny likes to drink, she decided to have a straight party and wanted me to help her plan it. Her theme was the song, "New York, New York."

We decorated different rooms in her house like New York City: goldfish in the bathtub represented the Fulton Fish Market; another room was Radio City Music Hall; a lot of play money on the walls in one room represented Wall Street. There were all kinds of kids at this party, kids who would normally be drinking and doing drugs. But nobody seemed to mind that the party was straight, and it ended up being a very good time.

It's not always easy to do positive things. I get discouraged. And sometimes I fail. I am just a normal kid with normal problems and hang-ups. Yet I think that being a good friend—helping my group of friends do what's right and have a good, "straight" time—is worth the mistakes and the effort. I believe anybody can do the things I've done—and more.

PEER PRESSURE

Darien's Orange and Blue

Rob Wilkins

MAKING A (GROUP) DIFFERENCE

Finally, we round this section off with a story about an ambulance crew in Darien, Connecticut, that is run completely by kids. This story proves that peers can not only build positive relationships, but that they make a big difference.

It could be just another teenage hangout. There is a steady stream of orange-and-blue jackets and talk of the senior trip. "Wheel of Fortune" is on the tube, and the host's big, perfect white teeth sparkle at the audience. The contestant, with big, white eyes, is yelling: "This is the happiest day of my life." The bleating voice of Stevie Nicks bleeds through a door down the hall.

There is not much excitement on this particular Friday night. Allison is in a back room doing homework. J.R. is talking about the Grateful Dead. Virginia is eating a ham sandwich. Jeb is rapping.

For the moment, they fight boredom.

The next moment, perhaps, becomes a matter of life and death.

At 11:49 P.M., long after TV hero Matt Houston had saved someone from jumping off a building, and while the dishes were being done, the call comes in. A lady is having trouble breathing.

Instant action. Barked commands. Instinctive moves. Adrenaline pumping. Screaming ambulance.

For fifty teenagers in the near-coastal town of Darien, Connecticut, this is a normal evening. For these teens run the ambulance service, from top to bottom. Some adults are part of the crew and some give advice, but no votes can be cast by anyone over the age of eighteen.

About twenty of the fifty teens are emergency medical technicians; the other thirty are in the process of completing the necessary 120 hours of training. Another fifty teens are on the waiting list.

They are known as Explorer Post 53 Emergency Medical Service (EMS). It is the only ambulance service in the country operated exclusively by teenagers.

Only those who are intelligent, cool under pressure, and responsible can get into the organization. They are the cream of the crop. Once in, each member gets an orange-and-blue jacket. That means prestige. It also means pressure, tremendous commitment, long hours, no pay, hard study, some boredom, and the opportunity to save lives.

The EMS in Darien got started because, among other things, Bud Doble hated his experience in the Boy Scouts. Too many slipknots and Popsicle sticks. So, when his son came to him and said he wanted to join the Cub Scouts, Doble made a decision. He became a scoutmaster. "I wanted it to become a good experience for him." Several other parents also joined.

A few years later, Doble's son, along with six other scouts, became an Eagle Scout. At that time Doble had another idea. It came from his long-time association with

PEER PRESSURE

medical services. He knew that what was desperately needed in the community, as well as the country, was a reputable ambulance service.

"The majority of ambulance service, up until ten years ago, was done by undertakers," Doble says. "They were the only ones with a vehicle that could carry a body in the horizontal position. In many cases that presented them with a conflict of interest. In fact, five years ago just about anyone could have operated an ambulance."

"Most of it was done by volunteers," Doble recalls. "Nice, well-meaning, but inept people. Anyone could have decided to start an ambulance service, put a red light on a wheelbarrow, go out on the thruway, and kill people."

So, Doble thought, why not use the Boy Scouts and "do it right"?

The seven Eagle Scouts became the nucleus of what now is Explorer Post 53 EMS. Under Doble's direction the organization set up rigid procedural and medical guidelines.

Some resistance to the EMS came from people who thought teenagers should stick to proms and clearing pimples. Doble ignored the criticism. "The kids quickly proved themselves. The medical profession [the surrounding hospitals] quickly adopted our programs. We had some resistance, but with the doctors and the hospitals 10,000 percent behind us, we just ignored the opposition."

Over the years, the EMS has earned an outstanding reputation, and many other organizations have copied their program. The awards clutter the wall, including a special achievement award from the American Medical Association—the only AMA award ever given for an ambulance service.

It has become, in fact, Darien's claim to fame. All three of the major network news programs have picked up the story. So have major magazines and newspapers. The mostly upper-class town of 22,000 has responded by supporting the EMS with more than enough money and praise.

Simply put, the EMS is considered one of the best in the country—teenagers or not.

But earning and maintaining a reputation does not happen by itself. There are no magical formulas or shortcuts. It takes hard work and sacrifice.

Rob Clark, president of the EMS and a senior at Darien High School, says the organization relies on a series of safeguards. Life-and-death decisions are not to be made by the half-committed or the ignorant or the weak-willed.

"They have to know just what they are getting into," Clark says. "From the outside, the organization is incredibly glamorous. But once you get in, you learn about the tremendous commitment. It has to be there."

Clark says a person has to be recommended for candidacy. "We just don't go out and ask for friends to join," he says. Once recommended, the person goes through a three-month training period that involves taking at least fifty hours of first-aid training. They also are asked to keep a strict schedule, do menial chores, and show compatibility. After the three months are over, a vote is taken whether or not to accept that person.

If accepted, there is more work. New members must complete 120 hours of training to qualify to become an advanced Emergency Medical Technician. Once these hours are completed, members may be asked to do them again. While working toward EMT status, they begin to do tasks for the squad—first as a radio dispatcher, then as a "rider" or a driver. Each task involves increased responsibility. They could be called out at any time of the night or day.

"It is a very tough and grueling process," Clark says. "It has to be."

Eventually, the hours of training come down to a few quick minutes during that crucial time after an accident when a life might hang in the balance. At that time, decisions must be instinctive.

Allison George remembers her first bad accident. She was a sophomore and a rider on the squad. As a rider, she was responsible for making sure the equipment was where it should be and helping to stabilize the victim.

It was night and raining. The victim was trapped and there was blood. A bad decision could have resulted in paralysis.

J.R. McDermott won't forget his first cardiac arrest. "You realize that this guy is lying there and he's really dead and you're trying to prolong his life. You are trying to get his heart to pump again."

They describe it as a swirl, remembered only after it's over: adrenaline and beeps and choking voices and blood and pressure and flashing lights.

"Generally speaking," McDermott says, "it all falls back on your training. If it is drilled into your head, you are going to know what to do automatically. You act on instinct. It is just beaten into you."

Back at the station, when the call is over, there are often long talks into the middle of the night.

Mostly about "what if."

The EMS orange-and-blue jackets—they wear them with pride. They are better than high-school letter sweaters. They are free. They cost a great deal.

"If someone sees you with one of these jackets on," says Allison, "they sometimes come up to you and thank you."

The jackets represent discipline, sacrifice, and, most of all, commitment.

"You have to be committed," Allison affirms. "With school and friends and family, you have to commit yourself. I've grown a lot because of the responsibility that I have had to handle. I've become more organized and disciplined. I think that the level of maturity [of the people in the EMS] is a cut above even most adults. It has to be."

"The adults in this town," Rob says, "don't look at us as teenagers. They look at us as young adults."

But all the hard work is worth it, they say. For at least one reason: They get to help others.

An example: A lady had an allergic reaction. She lost blood pressure. The ambulance was called. It was a difficult run. Quick thinking may have saved a life.

While at the hospital, one of the girls from the squad went to the lady to return her glasses.

"She just smiled and squeezed my hand and said thank you. That made me feel really good."

PEER PRESSURE

Being A Positive Peer

A Force for Good

Barbara Varenhorst

STRATEGIC THINKING

Barbara Varenhorst is a counselor who is responsible for setting up peer-counseling programs in public schools. In the following article she builds a practical strategy for being a positive peer.

Imagine two football guards shoving against each other. One's on the home team; one's an opponent. That's *pressure*.

Then there's peer pressure: Two guys, two girls, meet each other. One tries to nudge the other into doing something. Often, peer pressure forces you to act a certain way. It forces you to *be* a certain way. It forces you to act out of your own fears of being rejected and ridiculed. It forces you to act out of your desire and longing to be respected by others—by the group.

Without these fears or longings, peer pressure has no power. If you can kill the fears, you cure the problem. It's that simple. It's that hard.

Values . . . the inner stuff you treasure as important. "Your morals" is a good way to put it. What you actually do

PEER PRESSURE

When Fads clash.

determines what you value. If you drink, you value that; if you don't drink, you value that. Are you willing to give up, say, drinking, for personal satisfaction? Are you willing to keep drinking for, say, group satisfaction? What you are willing to give up or not give up, what you are willing to do or not do—those things determine your values. Strong personal values can counteract peer pressure.

But there is more than one kind of peer pressure. When we speak of peer pressure we naturally think of negative peer pressure. We all know what that is; we've experienced it in our lives, we've seen it at work. The word to sum it up is *harmful*—potentially harmful—to you or to others.

However, there are two other kinds of peer pressure. One is neutral peer pressure, where its effects on us are neither good nor bad. Consider the way we dress, the things we buy, our acceptance of fads to avoid being labeled as "different" or "old-fashioned." All these can be neutral peer pressures. They make no permanent stamp on our lives and future—unless we believe our worth as a person depends on outward appearances or possessions. If this happens, neutral peer pressure turns into very negative peer pressure.

There also is positive peer pressure. This peer pressure motivates us to act in positive ways. It draws its force from our good values, from our desire to earn self-respect and the respect of others for all the right reasons. Positive peer pressure brings out our strengths rather than our weaknesses. And, in turn, positive peer pressure builds the strengths of those who use it.

But here's the catch: Positive peer pressure is the least practiced of any of the three types of peer pressure. Is this because we don't truly believe we can have such influence on our peers? Or is it because we don't know how to pull it off? Whatever the reason, the following is a strategy for making peer pressure work positively for you.

MAKE THE NEGATIVES WORK FOR YOU

Dealing with negative peer pressure is one of the most effective ways of helping others act in a right way. When you refuse to give in to a group, you often shock or shame others into putting a halt to bad actions. What you do may provide the courage others need to follow your example. Consider Les.

As a senior in high school, Les was short, not very muscular, but a good enough athlete to have finally made the first-string basketball team. He also finally had been accepted by the bigger guys because of his skill on the court. Rumor had it, though, that he was the only virgin on the team—and some thought they should correct that. So they planned a party.

When Les arrived, they brought out a girl and told him

PEER PRESSURE

that now was his opportunity. Les was stunned. When he saw the smiles on their faces and all their eyes on him, Les agonized over what he should do. He didn't want to become the laughingstock of everyone or to lose their friendship. He thought about the values he had been taught by his parents, and those he had accepted as a Christian. He also thought how he would feel about himself if he gave in and used this girl in this way.

Struggling and stammering, he finally said, "I can't do this . . . I won't do it," and turned to leave. The silence that followed was finally broken when one of the guys said, "Les, I've never had a sexual experience either." Another mumbled the same thing, and then the party broke up.

That night, personal characters were shaped—imperceptibly, but permanently. Les found it was a turning point in his life. With that one critical decision, he was forced to choose the kind of person he wanted to be. From then on he found it easier to say no to negative pressure.

Perhaps others that night were affected in the same way. And perhaps the team as a whole worked and played together with a higher morale. The point is that this kind of positive peer pressure is a healing force, not a destroying one.

When faced with negative pressure, here are four points to remember and use:

1. *Know your values.* Making thoughtful decisions about the kind of person you want to be before you experience negative pressure is the best defense you can develop. Take Les. He, not the group, was in control of the situation. By having your own values thought out beforehand, you are more prepared to act as you want to act—not as the group wants you to act. Make up your own mind; guide your own decisions.

When confronted by negative peer pressure, ask yourself how you will feel about yourself afterward. What do you stand to gain or lose? This is one time when you *should* think of yourself first, rather than worrying about what others think of you. Remember, you always have to live with yourself, for the tomorrows and the years to come.

2. *You have rights!* Giving in to negative peer pressure is giving away your personal decisions. When you do this, you are allowing others to use you for their own purposes. If they were true friends, they wouldn't use you in this way. Friends never want you to do something that might harm you or that you don't want to do.

Remember, people are to be loved, and things are to be used. It is also true that no one really values someone who can be used, manipulated, or pressured. For a while they may fake friendship, but in the end they will feel they can toss you aside when you are no longer useful to them. If you don't want to be used, then hold on to your own decisions.

3. *Say no without turning others off.* It is amazing how difficult it is to comfortably say, "No, I don't want to do that." It actually helps to practice saying those words out loud when you are alone, listening to yourself and the tone of voice you use. Being able to do this in a quiet but firm manner avoids sounding self-righteous or judgmental. We don't need to judge others or to lay a guilt trip on anyone. But we do have the right to our own values and decisions. Les's "I can't do this" must have been said firmly, but apparently he didn't say it in a way that alienated his teammates. Rather, they respected him.

Sara learned this point the hard way. When she would go to high-school parties where kids were drinking, Sara refused to drink by saying, "I'm a Christian and Christians shouldn't be breaking the law." Obviously, her friends were turned off and began labeling her a "goody-goody." Eventually they didn't want to be around her. When she realized what she had been doing, she talked to her mother and decided all she really needed to say was "No, thank you. I don't care to have a drink." When she had future opportunities and did refuse in this way, she found her friends accepted it—and her. Some even admitted they admired her for being able to do this, and that it gave them courage to do the same.

4. *Change your group of friends.* If you find you are frequently being pressured by your friends to do things that are negative, perhaps you need to switch groups. Friendships are supposed to be relaxing and fun, not the source of constant battles. It takes energy to make the decisions forced on you by negative pressures. And that is valuable energy that could be put into more productive things, including really having fun. Finding a new group of friends is a heavy step to take, because it's hard, but in the end it will be worth it.

Take Doug, for instance. Doug made that decision when he was in the tenth grade. He couldn't take the way his group of friends were excluding others and treating those who were not part of their group. So he dropped the group and, as a result, was excluded by everyone. Being a good student and athlete, he just concentrated on his studies and sports. That's about all he did for two years. He didn't become bitter or try to fight back. He remained friendly and maintained a quiet confidence about his decision.

Early in his senior year things started to change. Students began hanging around him, even coming to him for advice. Eventually he was elected to some school leadership positions. At graduation time he was chosen by his fellow students for the Caring Student Scholarship. Students on the selection committee commented on how he had been an example to them in different ways throughout those rough years. One student summarized the feelings of all when she said, "Doug is the most highly respected student in this school. There is no one who deserves this award more."

Doug probably never will know the number of classmates who were affected by the way he handled himself through this tough time in his life. He does know, however, what he did for himself. He figured out what kind of person he wanted to be, and his character grew because he was tested daily. He won a prize greater than the scholarship—greater than any kind of popularity: He won the values he built inside himself through remaining true to his convictions. Anything that valuable demands a price.

PRESSURE THE NEGATIVES OUT OF YOUR GROUP

It's a given: All of you would like to eliminate cliques in your schools or on your campuses. Most of you wish that you and your classmates would be less cruel to others. You'd like to throw out the labels, stop the gossip. You would, because you know how it hurts.

A few of you have found how good it feels to go out of your way to do something kind or helpful for a classmate, such as sticking up for someone when he or she is being cut down. You've found personal satisfaction in including someone who doesn't have many friends.

But most often you feel you fail to use positive peer pressure. You think that people and groups can't be changed, or you don't think you can do anything about what's happening. Where would you start? Where do you get the courage?

Well, the bottom line is that groups *can* change, and you and your friends can bring that change about! Here are four steps to take to help the process along:

1. *Stamp out your own negatives.* If you can't do anything else, you can stop yourself from doing hurtful things to others. Stop your own labeling of others, cut out your own use of unkind names (even the printable ones like "stupid" and "nerd"). Vow not to listen to or pass along gossip. Gossip is a poisonous venom that harms not only

the target, but also the one who spreads it. Avoid making critical judgments of others.

You may not think these simple acts will make any difference, but it is amazing how powerfully they work to set an example for and inject trust into a group.

2. *Ask others to be positive.* It is remarkable how seldom we simply ask others to be positive. And it is equally remarkable how often they are jolted into responding to what you ask. The way you ask, of course, is critical. A command such as "Quit doing that!" will result in more anger and resentment than change. A comment such as "Since I don't like to be called names, and I don't think you do either, shouldn't we stop using them ourselves?" is much more effective.

I remember a time in college that affected me deeply. During a test a classmate broke the silence with, "May I remind everyone that this test is being taken under the Honor Code?" I don't know what triggered that announcement, but I can still feel the wave of "honor" that flowed through me, making it unthinkable for me to even consider cheating. The fact that I remember it illustrates how significant a comment from a classmate can be.

3. *Do something positive for others.* People really want to do positive things for others. This has been demonstrated many, many times in the peer counseling program I started for junior and senior high-school students. Often, though, it takes someone with an idea to organize a group to put it into action. For example, why not experiment with a "compliment campaign"? Get a group of friends together to agree to compliment a classmate or a teacher once a day for at least a month.

Set the ground rule that it has to be an honest, sincere compliment. Prepare one another for the negative reactions you probably will get as you do this. You'll get reactions ranging from remarks such as "You've got to be kidding" to no reaction at all. People often take compliments awkwardly.

Talk with your group of friends about how you can give compliments casually, without calling attention to yourself or the other person. It might be a casual comment while leaving class, such as, "Nice job on that report today, Kevin," or "Dr. Weeks, that was an interesting lecture today," or "Sally, that color looks great on you."

Once a week share your experiences and evaluate how the experiment is working. Maybe you won't see any obvious results, but at least you can know you're doing something positive.

Once, as part of youth group class, I organized the students into small groups and asked them to take turns being the one to receive a compliment from every other person in the group. The rules were that the compliment had to be sincere and that the one receiving it could not deny it, laugh, or do anything but thank the person giving the compliment.

Even though some of the students only knew one another through the youth group, each found something positive to say about every other person in their circle. It was exciting to see the effects, including the blushes, as compliments were received. Everyone left the meeting smiling. And I heard from their parents how much it had meant to the kids. Three months later they were still talking about it.

The result of a compliment may not be dramatic, but if even one person feels better about himself or herself, you have introduced positive pressure to your peers.

4. *Organize to change your school.* The Palo Alto high schools in California were the first to use the peer counseling program I developed. Over a period of years it became evident that many of the drug, truancy, and academic problems in those schools began during the ninth grade, when students were making the transition from middle school. In searching for a solution, the idea emerged of

using upperclassmen as buddies to these students. It was called the Friendship Club.

Juniors and seniors were recruited from every group on the campus. In recruiting students, I was overwhelmed by the number and variety of positive reactions I got and the willingness of the kids to participate. Realizing that many students need to learn basic friendship skills before they are able to reach out to others, I provided two days of training in August.

The weekend before school started, each student called the two buddies they had been assigned. At that time they made arrangements to meet during the first day of school. After that it was up to each pair as to when they would meet and what they would do. Students were expected to keep contact with their younger buddy for the entire ninth-grade year. The upperclassmen met as a group two evenings a month to talk about how things were going and to get help with any problems they might be having.

Not all the teams worked out, but few students gave up. One boy reported that he had ended up studying with his ninth-grade buddy every night, just to get the kid to do his homework. "I don't know how it's helping him," he remarked with a smile, "but *my* grades sure have improved." Most teams just did fun things together after school or on weekends, out of which grew some lasting friendships.

Other ninth graders who didn't have a buddy began to request one, even as late as April and May. Gradually the message got around that upperclassmen are a helpful resource rather than people to be feared. Teachers and principals also began to see the effects. Fewer behavior problems were reported, even among students who weren't involved. There were fewer fights on campus and fewer ninth graders sent to the district's Discipline Committee.

The following year the idea was extended to form a Special Friendship Club for students in the Educable Mentally Retarded (EMR) class housed on campus. First, several students signed up to act as tutors daily in the EMR class. All were paired with an EMR student as a special buddy. The group then started planning and carrying out a variety of club social activities.

The group went bowling, Christmas shopping, miniature golfing, and cross-country skiing together. With the help of two special buddies for each EMR student, the previously nonskiing EMR students eventually were able to go sailing over hills and trails. One girl developed a close relationship with her EMR buddy, and they talked each night at length on the phone. One EMR student who loved sports regularly visited the soccer practices and games to watch his buddy, and so became a friend to the entire team.

Who gains the most from these friendship activities? Everyone benefits in some way. This school now is a friendlier school with fewer cliques. The lives of some ninth graders got off to a positive start in high school, and now these students feel better about themselves. EMR students have grown in their social skills because of their contacts with their special buddies.

But those who are giving their friendship are the ones who gain the most. In working together with classmates from other groups or cliques, they are learning to tear down the walls of judgment and labeling that separate groups from one another. They are experiencing the satisfaction that comes from thinking less about themselves and becoming involved in the lives of others. Some find they have fewer problems themselves because this has become an antidote for boredom and insecurity—the two main causes of negative peer pressure.

Negative peer pressure will always be part of our lives. It will serve as a test of who we really are and who we are becoming. Positive peer pressure, however, is not one of life's certainties. It will exist only as a result of deliberate effort by people who care about the world they live in. It, too,

PEER PRESSURE

is a test—a test of our courage, our belief in ourselves, and our belief in others.

When you use positive peer pressure you will find that you develop a friendship with yourself. You also will discover a deeper, richer quality in all your relationships. This is a prize worth going for—and as you do so, more and more of your peers will be convinced of the power positive pressure holds to change their lives.

JOURNAL entry✔

Check *one* possibility

... to change a bad situation to something better.

☐ If your friends edge somebody out of the group, have lunch with this person.

☐ If your friends gossip about somebody, simply say, "I don't want to talk about her anymore. I really don't think it's right."

☐ If two friends in your group are fighting, talk to each one individually, away from the group, about the problem.

☐ Get interested in some friend's activity or hobby.

☐ Send a birthday, Halloween, Christmas, St. Patrick's Day (or whatever holiday is close) card to someone in your school who is not considered popular.

☐ Talk to one of your teachers about tutoring an underclassman in a subject you are good at.

Today's Date: _____

PEER PRESSURE

How to Influence Friends (and Win People)

Jim Long

OTHERS NEED YOU

More often than not, we think of the thug-types in "Sandpiper" as the norm for peer pressure—people pouring it on from the negative side, always making a bad situation worse.

When you start thinking such people have the power to influence you, remember that you have power, too. Get them before they get you—just get them with goodness. In the next article, Jim Long, writer of *Campus Life's* Bible-oriented "Spark" column, gives us some tips from the Bible for building better friendships.

The New Testament says, "Let us consider how we may spur one another on toward love and good deeds" (Hebrews 10:24). We are individuals who have the power to affect other people. We should use our influence with others to help them be more loving and good. Try the following:

1. *Find someone who's down*—discouraged, grieving, or just down on his luck. You may not have all the answers (or *any* of the answers), but your expressions of friendship and concern can be enormously encouraging.

2. *Find someone who is joyful.* The Bible says to weep with those who weep, but it also says to rejoice with those who rejoice (Romans 12:15). We need to shake our feelings of jealousy when things go well for someone else, and let that person know we're glad for him or her.

3. *Find someone who is weak.* You might notice someone struggling with compromise, giving in to what he or she feels is wrong. Sometimes those "sins of compromise" are really calls for friendship. Ever wonder what would happen if you struck up such a friendship? Maybe you should find out.

4. *Find someone who is strong.* We can't always be the strong ones. We need to find friends whose confidence and advice we value. Not only will we be helped by leaning on these friends, but having us lean on them will make them stronger, more conscientious.

Face it, you need others. We all do.

"Let us not give up meeting together, as some are in the habit of doing, but let us encourage one another" (Hebrews 10:25).

We *are* individuals, but groups are good, too. It's sometimes hard to sort out life when you're alone. You need the help of friends when you are weak (and even when you are strong), especially friends who share your values, friends who will use their influence for your good.

5. *Get involved in friendships with a purpose.* Talk with one or two of your closest friends and suggest you meet regularly to talk about your good times and bad times. Pray together, and pray individually, for each other.

6. *Get involved in a club*—one such as Campus Life,

Young Life, or Student Venture. These groups offer varied programs of good times, serious discussion, and friendship.

7. *Get involved in a local church.* It helps to have caring friends of all ages. A good church can provide such friends, as well as help in understanding your faith.

8. *Get involved with your family.* Often the last people we share our serious concerns with are the people we are closest to. It shouldn't be that way. Take that first step in serious conversation: Talk to your mom or dad, or a brother or sister. Let them know that you count on their support and that they can count on yours.

Don't be afraid to be an individual. Remember, you can be a positive influence in the lives of others. But you also need friends to help you. Choose wisely.

A Question of Belonging

Jim Long

HOW CAN GOD HELP ME BELONG?

Belonging. Fitting in. That's where we began this book, with Trey, Mike, Shannon, Deena, and, of course, David. And so, as we close this book about bad and good peer pressure, we turn again to that special need we all have to belong. But we close not just by looking at peers. We close by looking beyond peers—to God's plan for building lasting friendships. Jim Long shows us how our need to belong relates to God, and his special group of friends: the church.

I suppose Harvey, as well as anyone, knew the pain of belonging. And not belonging. Not that he wasn't nice. If anything, he may have been too nice. Harvey was a goody-goody.

He was tall for his age, not fat, but ample. His hair was cropped so close you could see the geography of his skull, every hill and valley. His beige skin showed through his light-blond hair with an almost luminescent quality.

He often seemed disoriented, like he wasn't quite sure

what was going on around him. He would tilt his head, straining to listen, and squint his eyes into thin, inquisitive slits. And, as if to complete an already quirky image, Harvey played the accordion.

Even today when I think of in-groups and out-groups, cliques and belonging, I think first of Harvey. Odd Harvey. Out-of-place Harvey. I picture Harvey when I think of belonging because it was through him that I learned something about myself. Something very uncomfortable. Something that still bothers me.

To be sure, Harvey was peculiar. Yet what I remember him for, as much as anything, was how kind he was. He expressed his kindness in little things. For instance, he always showed up with a complete lunch, not like the boring brown bag I packed. And he shared it. No big fanfare—just, "Have a Twinkie," or, "Try this sandwich."

Our conversations were always rather low-key. I never felt I had to try to impress Harvey—he didn't even care about the things that impressed everyone else—so there was a naturalness about our friendship that made it easy to talk and listen. Besides, we had known each other since second grade and had spent a lot of time together growing up.

It was only as I got older that it began to dawn on me that Harvey didn't quite fit the norm. My other friends laughed at him, even mimicked him. I started to feel uneasy about eating lunch with him, wondering who was going to see me and what they'd think. Gradually, an almost paranoid self-consciousness settled over this long-standing friendship, though, I suppose, Harvey never noticed it.

One day early in my sophomore year, a Wednesday as I recall, I couldn't handle the embarrassment any longer so I just didn't show up at lunch. I went with some other friends instead. I did feel guilty, like I was betraying a friendship, but after all, Harvey was weird and I didn't want to be branded as weird, too. I even felt guilty the next day when I

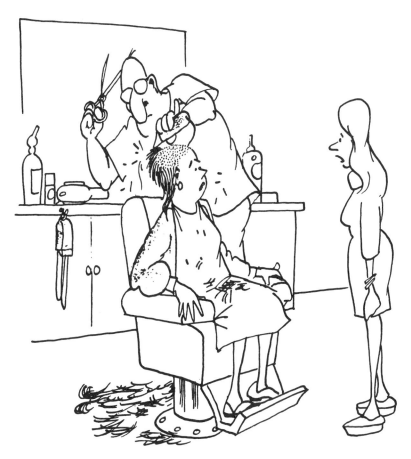

OH, NO! I'M TOO LATE! I JUST TALKED TO TRACY AND IT TURNS OUT IT'S JUST THE BOYS WHO ARE HAVING IT DONE!

PEER PRESSURE

again snubbed him. In fact, that guilt persisted at least a week.

I never did talk to Harvey about it. I just avoided him. I avoided him at lunch. I avoided him before and after school. I felt too guilty. Besides, I was enjoying my "normal" friendships and I wasn't willing to change.

In time I pretty much forgot about Harvey. Until my senior year. The final semester was drawing toward a conclusion, and my high-school career along with it. I recall a beautiful, warm April afternoon—typical of southern California—when the temperature was well into the seventies. Brilliant sunlight washed over the campus. I walked across the quad at lunchtime, alone, but in rather buoyant spirits. The open area was alive with activity; it was the principal place students gathered at lunchtime. Their laughter and talking rose and fell in sort of a pleasant cacophony, typical of high-school lunch hours.

I bisected the quad diagonally and continued down an outdoor hallway toward my locker. Then I turned right, onto a north-south sidewalk. Here it was quiet, empty. Totally deserted. Except for one solitary figure. Toward the end of the hallway, sitting on the sidewalk, with his back against the brick building, was Harvey. After more than two years of lunch hours, he was still eating alone. I don't think I have ever seen a lonelier looking person. And as I walked past him and glanced down, he didn't even look up.

I'M OK, YOU'RE OK

I guess it's a commentary on my own insensitivity that I readily set aside that pathetic image of "weird Harvey" without so much as a consoling word. But now, in retrospect, I remember Harvey and wonder what it was that was so important to me that I was willing to sacrifice a friendship, even that friendship. Then I realized I wanted exactly what I was denying Harvey: a sense of belonging, a sense of being a part of something larger than myself. I felt awkward, insecure, and so I went on the hunt to find a group that would say, "You're okay." In my mind, Harvey threatened all that so he had to go. I certainly didn't want the fallout from his weirdness raining down on me.

It would be nice if groups were more open; if we all agreed, "Well, Harv is a bit different, but there's room for everybody. No one should be shut out." But who wants to be open? If I am open I have to learn how to deal with all kinds of people who are different, people I hesitate to befriend. So I interact with only the comfortable people. The safe people.

I think of my insensitivity toward Harvey and conclude: Belonging was tremendously important to me. And the question is not simply, "Will I create an open, safe spot for weirdos and rejects?" Rather, the more unnerving question is: "If I do welcome the 'weirdos,' will the others, the 'normal' people, still accept me?"

UNMASKING THE LONE RANGER

I've thought a lot about belonging, the fairness of it, the unfairness. And I wonder, is it really wrong to want to belong, to fear being excluded?

We certainly seem to be wired for interaction, as if the idea of flying life solo is naturally alien. In fact, you get funny, suspicious feelings about the person who has no regard for what people think of him. That Lone Ranger mentality just doesn't fit with the way life feels.

I wonder, too, is it really wrong to form groups of people with whom we naturally identify?

What would happen if you yanked some guy out of the auto shop, tossed in a clarinet player from the marching band, added a soprano from the choir, then, for good measure, included three computer whiz-kids and perhaps a history buff?

Now imagine that one is an Italian who grew up in New

York City and another is a trendy southern California transplant with a totally different vocabulary. There might also be a Chicano, an inner-city black, a suburbanite rich kid, and a guy from Texas (complete with cowboy boots and hat). From a faith standpoint, one is agnostic, another a Jew. One person is proud of his Catholicism, one a staunch Baptist from a strict home, and yet another is a tongues-speaking charismatic.

With such diversity around us, it's surprising any two people ever get along. Furthermore, if I don't quite feel secure about myself, and I'm looking for friends who will obligingly buttress my sagging ego, am I really going to group with people I don't understand, people I don't agree with, people whose worlds are radically different from mine?

A certain amount of like grouping with like is inevitable, even good.

PROBLEM ONE: THE EXPECTATIONS OF OTHERS

Many of the group's expectations are healthy. But groups tend to run wild, adding all kinds of secondary demands that turn out to be suffocating (if for no other reason than because they are so ridiculously unnecessary).

Tucked away in the Old Testament (1 Samuel 16:7) is the truism, "Man looks at the outward appearance, the LORD looks at the heart." Our passport into God's understanding and acceptance is not a funny, fabric alligator or a Members Only tag. God sees deeper than all that. Groups can be so superficial, and acceptance rituals are as shallow as a certain kind of talk or a wearing of stripes instead of checks—this week. It's true, people do look on the outward appearance. And often they are looking for the wrong things.

Which leads us to . . .

PROBLEM TWO: CATERING TO OTHER PEOPLE

The expectations others place on me are their problem. Catering to those expectations, playing the group game, is *my* problem. I sense that God also has expectations of me, but they are vastly different from most of the group's; God's expectations are always healthy and helpful.

When I decided to exclude Harvey, bulldozing his feelings in order to find acceptance with people who colored him odd, I violated basic Christian ideas. Good ideas. Ideas about love. And my New Testament asks me, "Do you seek to please people, or God?"

Which raises the question of . . .

PROBLEM THREE: WRONG GOALS

I wonder, had I felt more confident, would I have urged my friends to include Harvey, to look beyond his superficial quirks and see his kindness? It would have been a good goal: Find friends for Harvey.

At the same time, it would have seemed an outrageous idea. I had my hands full trying to create and service my own friendships. My friends had their work cut out for them, too, manufacturing and warehousing their "normal" friendships. We were all insecure.

If I feel insecure and try to pull my sense of identity— who I am—from belonging to the group, I throw myself open to becoming something I don't really want to be. Or shouldn't be. In this case, a selfish, insensitive person. Why trust the group to define the real me?

And that leads to . . .

PROBLEM FOUR: GROUP THINKING

You could call this "Leadership by Intimidated Consensus." Have you noticed that the demands and standards of a group often are different from the individual preferences of the group members?

A friend of mine got the bright idea of racing down Workman Mill Road at the foot of southern California's Whittier Hills. It was a stretch of winding road you'd hardly consider ideal for high-speed traffic. There were four of us in two cars, who, with silly grins on our faces, all agreed, "Sure, Jerry, that's a great idea."

Later, paste-white and shaking following a near-miss, head-on, three-car pileup, we asked each other, "Did *you* really want to do that?" In a rare moment of honesty we had to admit that none of us wanted to do many of the things we all agreed to do. We were just too intent on impressing one another. A typical, group-thinking approach.

All of us do things that we don't really want to do and wouldn't choose to do if we were alone. This fact has an interesting twist: People often greatly respect the one person who simply stands up and says, "No, that's not what I want to do." The film *Chariots of Fire* highlighted Eric Little's resolve, "I won't run on Sunday," as an example of standing for convictions. People often want to live differently but are just too fearful to do so. Still, there are those times. Times when one person honors his conscience, adheres to his convictions . . . and others follow his lead. Or at least respect the gumption he showed.

And I wonder, why not make caring a conviction? And then stand for it.

HOW ABOUT SWITCHING GROUPS?

When I decided to become a Christian, I had this odd idea that I was executing the most brilliantly independent feat. I was beating the system. I was putting people, with all their group-belonging demands, in their place. I didn't need the affirmation of all those other people; I had the capital G on my side.

Surprise! God alone wasn't enough . . . almost, but not quite. I still felt uneasy when people didn't wave my flag. I still felt lonely when things at home depressed me. I still hung back cautiously when confronted with bona fide "weirdos"—that is, anyone substantially different from me.

I got this uneasy feeling, this embarrassed guilty feeling: Suppose Harvey waltzed back into my circle of friends? Would I feel any more inclined to welcome him? Or would I freeze him out once again?

I had good reason to wonder. It was a group of church friends, I recall, that put Mary in her place—out the door. Mary had a reputation for being a bit loose, for doing out in the open the kinds of things the rest of us were all eager to do in the dark. So all of us moral people huddled around the back row of the church and said nasty things about "Dirty Mary."

And it worked. We not only kept her out of our tight, little in-group, we drove her away from the church. I had seen it firsthand; being "Christian" did not at all guarantee a warm welcome to the weird of the world. So I have this marvelous idea, a great way to think of Christianity. But I wonder, will we let it work?

The idea is simple: Shouldn't becoming a Christian be like switching peer groups? You could decide, "I want to be a Christian. I believe in Jesus, but I'm not sure I can make it alone. I need the support of other people. I need a group I can belong to, a group to teach me what it means to be Christian, a group to support me when I decide I want to hang on to my convictions. And, in becoming a Christian, I join with other Christians to find the support I need."

It ought to happen.

After Jesus died, returned to life, and reentered heaven, the Christians quickly gained a reputation: "Look how much those people love one another!" People were astounded. It doesn't seem too much to ask that the same thing would happen today. If Weird Harvey becomes a

PEER PRESSURE

Christian, I should welcome him into the club, along with the clarinet player, the computer-brain, the Chicano, and the Texan.

The New Testament suggests we ought to consider how we can provoke one another to love and good works. That sounds like a fine assignment for a group.

GROUPS WITH HALOS?

As much as I like the Christian peer group idea, a caution strikes me. Human nature being what it is, wouldn't we soon treat Christianity the same way we treat any other peer group? In place of true convictions and love for God, would we simply do what we do and say what we say because it's what the other Christians expect? Instead of being children of God, would we become children of the Christian clique?

It is very easy—second nature, in fact—to do things, even right and good things, simply to please a Christian group. That brings us back to the group-thinking problem. People do things just to impress others. But there's better reason to do things: because they are right. And there's an excellent reason to avoid certain things: because they are wrong. That's different from doing them because everybody you know is a Christian and does those good things.

God shared his expectations in black and white—in the Bible. Then he passed the initiative to us. "Live life my way," I imagine him telling me, "not because others expect you to, but because *I* want you to, because I planned this better way for you." I enjoy thinking of God like that, as if he is the ultimate "group." I belong to him.

That's another way of saying that Christianity has to become a part of me. A group faith that is only a group faith is not good enough. If my faith doesn't become a part of me, I may resort to something foolish, like tossing it overboard when things get stormy with my peers. If my Christianity is just the group's Christianity, if it doesn't become a part of me, I may hang on to it for years and never really know why. I may one day hold it up to the light, stare at it, scratch my head, figure it's irrelevant, and put it on the shelf.

Maybe that's why the Bible uses a different image. Becoming a Christian goes far deeper than just signing up for a new peer group. Becoming a Christian means joining a new family, *God's* family. Other Christians, regardless of their oddities and quirks, are my brothers and sisters. This is not a loosely structured club of insecure people; the loyalties run deep and the bonds are permanent. I am free to be who I am, and I find support in a group of Christian friends. I need the best of both individuality and group support.

When I think of in-groups and out-groups, cliques and belonging, I think of my weird friend Harvey and the way I treated him. But I also visualize a long, narrow corridor, a drab gray sidewalk, and brown-red brick walls. At the end of the corridor, leaning against the wall, in place of Harvey, I see myself . . . alone. And I picture a form I identify as God, walking the length of the sidewalk. When he comes to me, he looks down, past my outward appearance, to see a person hung up with pleasing people. But he understands all that, and rather than offering a harsh rebuke, he reminds me of his invitation to belong to his family, and to welcome others.

About the YOUTHSOURCE™ Publishing Group

YOUTHSOURCE™ books, tapes, videos, and other resources pool the expertise of three of the finest youth-ministry resource providers in the world:

Campus Life Books—publishers of the award-winning *Campus Life* magazine, who for nearly fifty years have helped high schoolers live Christian lives.

Youth Specialties—serving ministers to middle-school, junior-high, and high-school youth for over twenty years through books, magazines, and training events such as the National Youth Workers Convention.

Zondervan Publishing House—one of the oldest, largest, and most respected evangelical Christian publishers in the world.

Campus Life	**Youth Specialties**	**Zondervan**
465 Gundersen Dr.	1224 Greenfield Dr.	1415 Lake Dr., S.E.
Carol Stream, IL 60188	El Cajon, CA 92021	Grand Rapids, MI 49506
708/260-6200	619/440-2333	616/698-6900